GRAPHIC LIBRARY

DISASTERS IN HISTORY

THE ATTACK ON PEARL HARBOR

by Jane Sutcliffe

illustrated by Bob Lentz

Consultant:

William L. O'Neill

Professor of History

Rutgers University

Capstone
press

Mankato, Minnesota

Graphic Library is published by Capstone Press,
1710 Roe Crest Drive, North Mankato, Minnesota 56003
www.capstonepub.com

Library of Congress Cataloging-in-Publication Data
Sutcliffe, Jane.
    The attack on Pearl Harbor / by Jane Sutcliffe ; illustrated by Bob Lentz.
    p. cm.—(Graphic library. Disasters in history)
    Includes bibliographical references and index.
    Audience: Ages 8–12.
    ISBN-13: 978-0-7368-5477-1 (hardcover)
    ISBN-10: 0-7368-5477-0 (hardcover)
    ISBN-13: 978-0-7368-6872-3 (softcover pbk.)
    ISBN-10: 0-7368-6872-0 (softcover pbk.)
    1. Pearl Harbor (Hawaii), Attack on, 1941—Comic books, strips, etc. I. Lentz, Bob. II. Title.
III. Series.
D767.92.S88 2006
940.54'26693—dc22   2005029862
Summary: In graphic novel format, tells the story of the bombing of Pearl Harbor on
    December 7, 1941, and the United States' reaction to the event.

Art Director and Designer
Bob Lentz

Editor
Donald Lemke

Special thanks to Dr. H. Todd Stradford, professor, University of Wisconsin-Platteville.

Editor's note: Direct quotations from primary sources are indicated by a yellow background.

Direct quotations appear on the following pages:
Pages 7, 14, from *Investigation of the Pearl Harbor Attack: Report Pursuant to S. Con. Res.
    27, 79th Congress* by U. S. Congress. Joint Committee on the Investigation of the Pearl
    Harbor Attack (Washington: U.S. Govt. Print. Off., 1946).
Pages 9, 19, from Gordon William Prange's interview with Commander Mitsuo Fuchida,
    December 10, 1963, as quoted in *December 7, 1941: The Day the Japanese Attacked Pearl
    Harbor* by Gordon William Prange (New York: McGraw-Hill, 1988).
Page 15, from a letter to Gordon William Prange from Robert G. Crouse, November 24, 1964,
    as quoted in *December 7, 1941: The Day the Japanese Attacked Pearl Harbor* by Gordon
    William Prange (New York: McGraw-Hill, 1988).
Page 17, from Gordon William Prange's interview with 1st Class Boatswain's Mate Howard C.
    French, August 11, 1964, as quoted in *December 7, 1941: The Day the Japanese Attacked
    Pearl Harbor* by Gordon William Prange (New York: McGraw-Hill, 1988).
Pages 24–25, from Franklin D. Roosevelt's *Joint Address to Congress Leading to a Declaration
    of War Against Japan*, December 8, 1941, archived at Franklin D. Roosevelt Presidential
    Library and Museum (http://www.fdrlibrary.marist.edu/oddec7.html).

TABLE OF CONTENTS

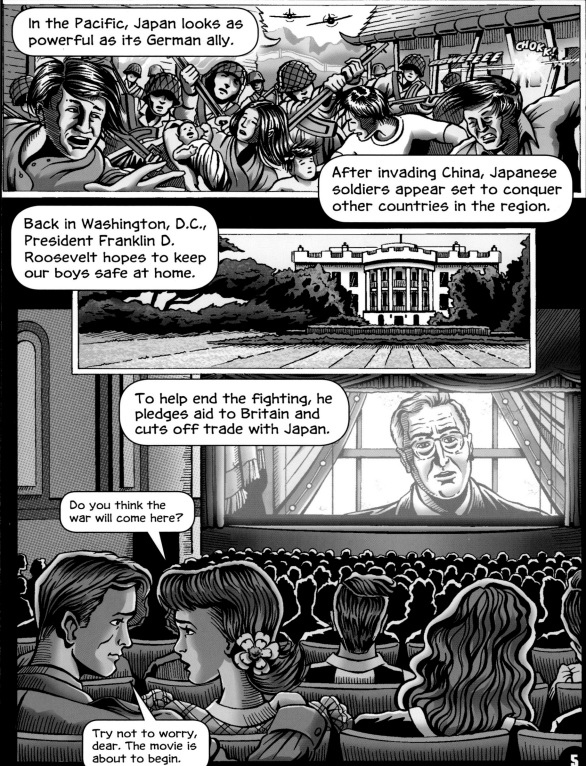

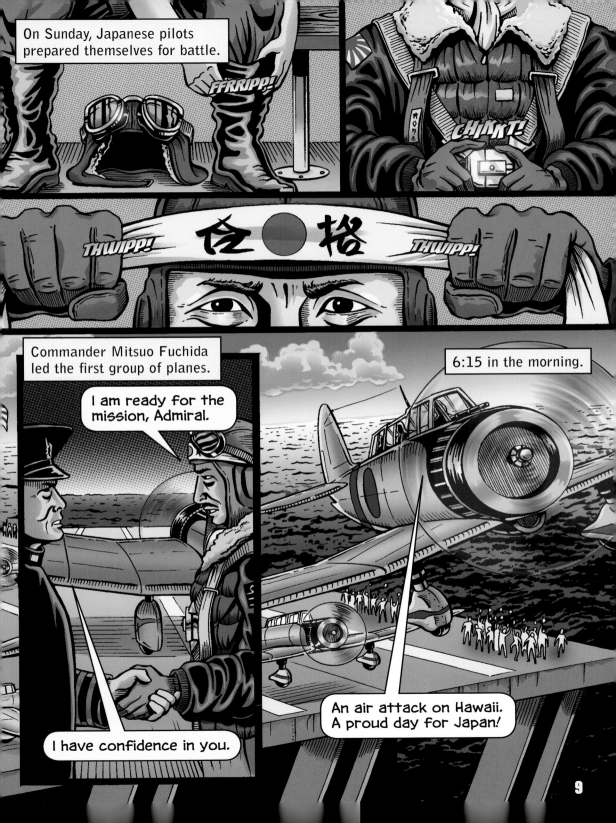

On Sunday, Japanese pilots prepared themselves for battle.

FFRRIPP!

CHIKKT!

THWIPP!   THWIPP!

Commander Mitsuo Fuchida led the first group of planes.

I am ready for the mission, Admiral.

I have confidence in you.

6:15 in the morning.

An air attack on Hawaii. A proud day for Japan!

9

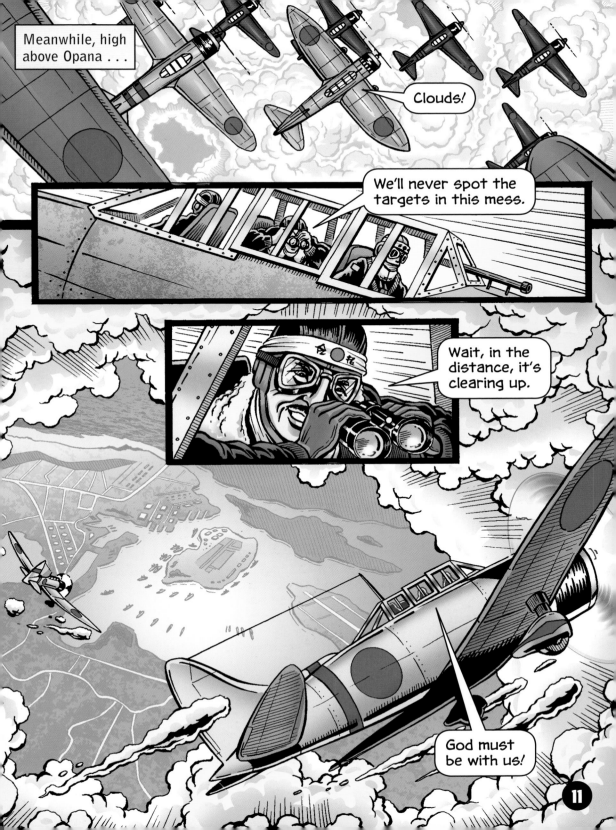

7:55 in the morning.

SCRREEEEE!

Admiral Nagumo, I have a message from Commander Fuchida.

トラ
(Tora!)

トラ
(Tora!)

トラ
(Tora!)

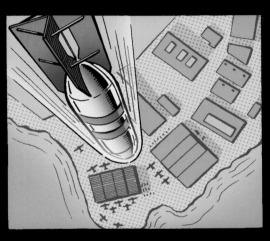

What does it say, Admiral?

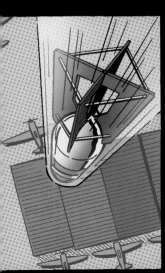

We've caught the Americans by surprise!

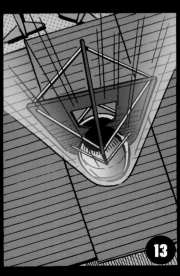

CHAPTER 3
BATTLE STATIONS!

As men raced to their battle stations, Japanese planes filled the skies. Explosions rocked the USS *California* . . .

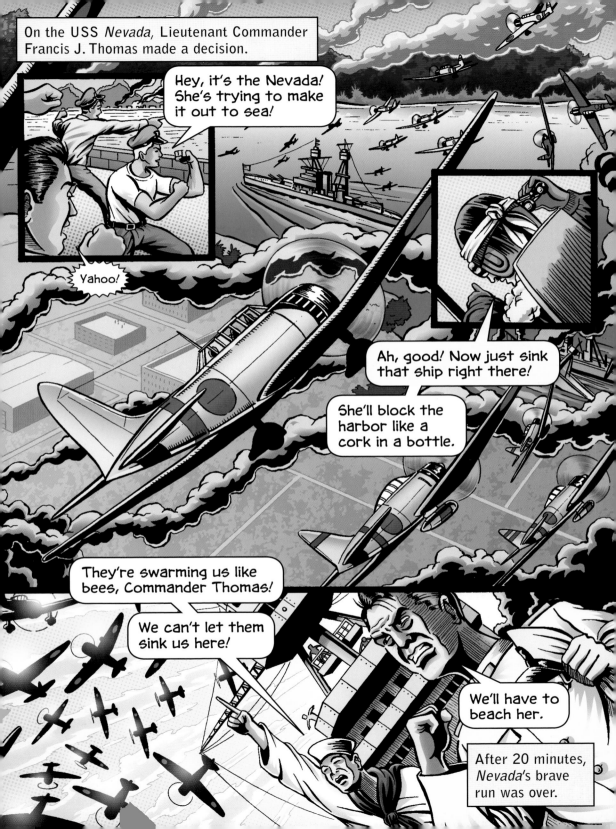

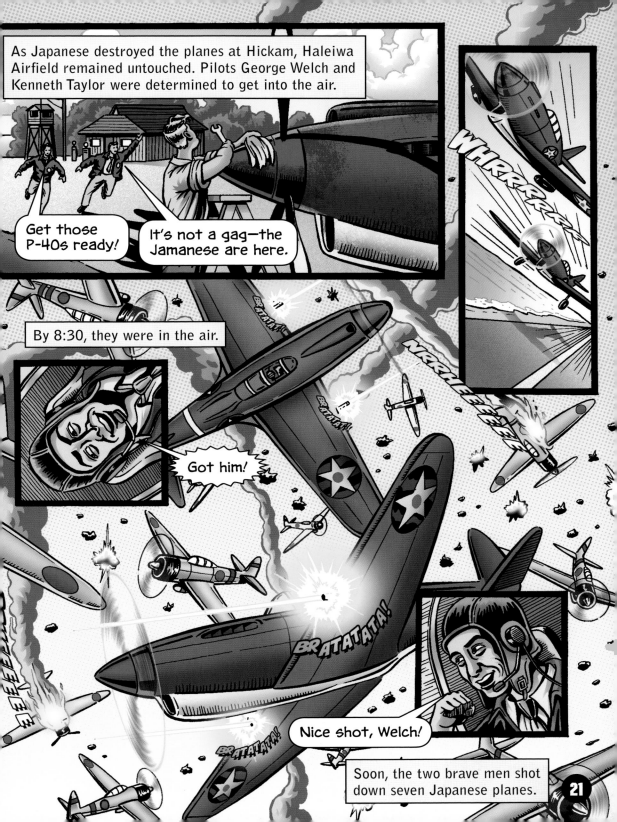

Meanwhile, the first Japanese planes left Pearl Harbor. Ten minutes later, a second group arrived. But this time . . .

. . . the Americans were ready to fight back.

BRAKA-BRAKA-BRAKA-BRAKA-BRAKA!!!

That's for the boys on the Arizona!

Chaplain, what are you doing here? You're not supposed to touch these weapons.

Well then, boys, praise the Lord and pass the ammunition!

He can say a prayer, can't he? Lord knows we need it.

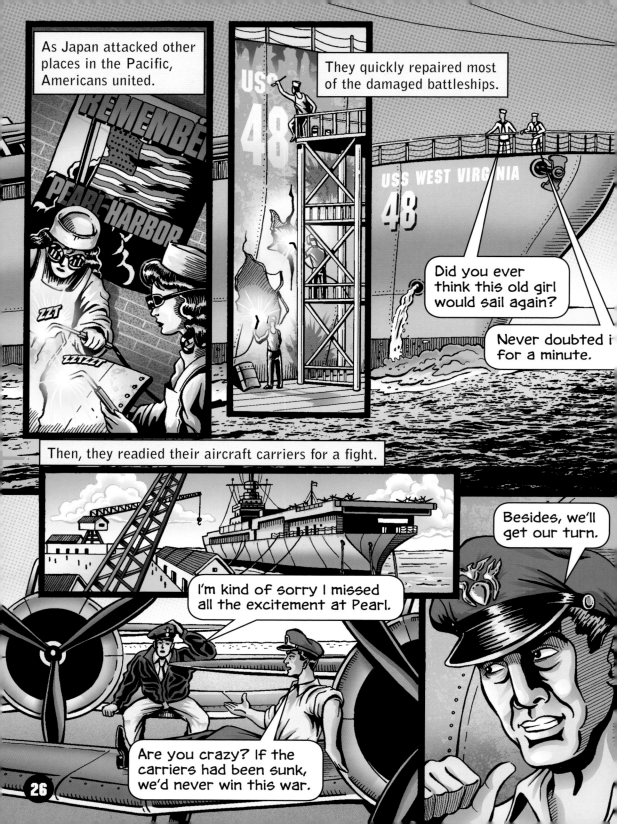

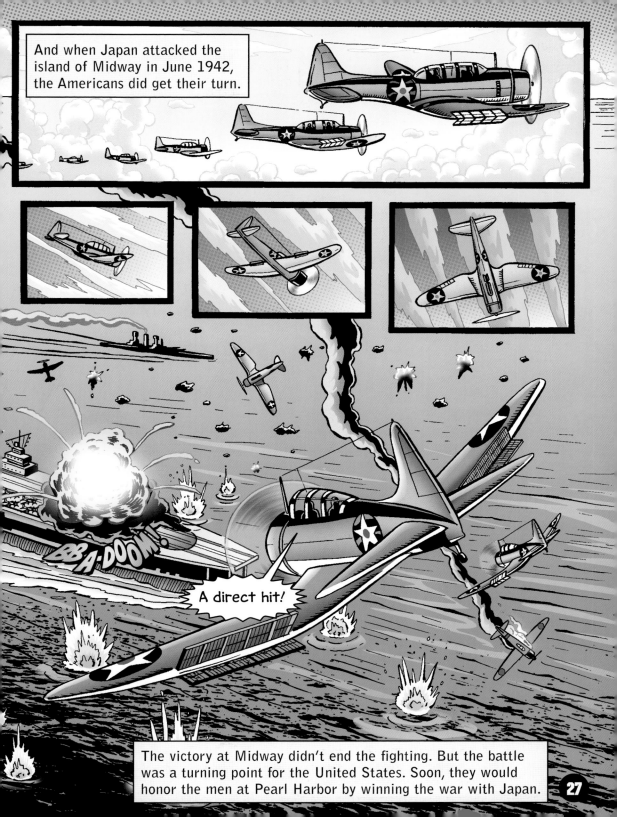

And when Japan attacked the island of Midway in June 1942, the Americans did get their turn.

A direct hit!

BBA-DOOM!

The victory at Midway didn't end the fighting. But the battle was a turning point for the United States. Soon, they would honor the men at Pearl Harbor by winning the war with Japan.

- Before flying to Pearl Harbor, each Japanese airman tied a white cloth called a *hachimaki* around his head. The symbol of the Rising Sun and Japanese words for "Sure Victory" marked the traditional bandanna. The Japanese wore a *hachimaki* when they were ready to die for their country.

- Surprisingly, the United States fired the first shot in the war with Japan. On December 7, at 6:45 in the morning, the crew of the USS *Ward* spotted a midget submarine heading for Pearl Harbor. The destroyer *Ward* sank the sub and reported the attack to Naval Headquarters. Unfortunately for the United States, no one took the report seriously.

- Like other militaries, Japanese forces often relayed messages in secret code. At 7:53 on December 7, Commander Fuchida sent out the message "*Tora, Tora, Tora*" to the Japanese fleet. The message, meaning "Tiger, Tiger, Tiger" in English, was secret code for surprise attack achieved.

- Before December 7, many U.S. officers believed Pearl Harbor couldn't be successfully attacked by air. They thought the harbor was too shallow for aerial torpedoes to work. The Japanese, however, had attached wooden tail fins to their torpedoes. The fins made aerial torpedoes a powerful weapon for Japan and devastated the U.S. Pacific Fleet.

- During the Japanese attack, Doris "Dorie" Miller was a cook aboard the USS *West Virginia.* As bombs rained down, Miller carried the ship's injured captain to safety. He then grabbed an anti-aircraft machine gun and started firing, even though he had no training. For his courage, Miller became the first African American to receive the Navy Cross. This honor is one of the highest awards for courage given by the U.S. military.

- After Pearl Harbor, Americans worried that people who looked Japanese were spies. In February 1942, President Roosevelt ordered all Japanese-Americans removed from their homes on the West Coast. Almost 120,000 people were sent to relocation camps. Many were held at these camps until near the end of World War II in 1945.

- In 1962, a national memorial opened at Pearl Harbor, Hawaii. The memorial rests above the sunken USS *Arizona*, which remains a tomb for hundreds of soldiers who died on December 7, 1941. Today, visitors can take a boat to the memorial and pay their respects to these fallen heroes.

GLOSSARY

dispatch (DIS-pach)—an important official message

infamy (IN-fuh-mee)—an extreme and publicly known criminal or evil act

liberty (LIB-ur-tee)—permission to be away from naval duty for a short time

lieutenant (lu-TEN-ent)—an officer in the navy

magazine (MAG-uh-zeen)—a room or building for storing ammunition or weapons

moor (MOR)—to tie up or anchor a boat

radar (RAY-dar)—a machine used to detect and locate objects such as enemy aircraft

INTERNET SITES

FactHound offers a safe, fun way to find Internet sites related to this book. All of the sites on FactHound have been researched by our staff.

Here's how:

1. *Visit www.facthound.com*
2. Type in this special code **0736854770** for age-appropriate sites. Or enter a search word related to this book for a more general search.
3. Click on the **Fetch It** button.

FactHound will fetch the best sites for you!

READ MORE

Adams, Simon. *World War II*. DK Eyewitness Books. New York: DK Pub., 2004.

Fitzgerald, Stephanie. *Pearl Harbor: Day of Infamy*. Snapshots in History. Minneapolis: Compass Point Books, 2005.

Pierce, Alan. *The Bombing of Pearl Harbor*. American Moments. Edina, Minn.: Abdo, 2005.

Tanaka, Shelley. *Attack on Pearl Harbor: The True Story of the Day America Entered World War II*. New York: Hyperion Books For Children, 2001.

BIBLIOGRAPHY

Lord, Walter. *Day of Infamy*. New York: H. Holt, 2001.

Prange, Gordon William. *At Dawn We Slept: The Untold Story of Pearl Harbor*. 60th Anniversary ed. New York: Penguin Books, 2001.

Prange, Gordon William. *December 7, 1941: The Day the Japanese Attacked Pearl Harbor*. New York: McGraw-Hill, 1988.

United States Congress. Joint Committee on the Investigation of the Pearl Harbor Attack. *Investigation of the Pearl Harbor Attack*. Washington: U.S. Govt. Print. Off., 1946.

INDEX

P9-DIW-919

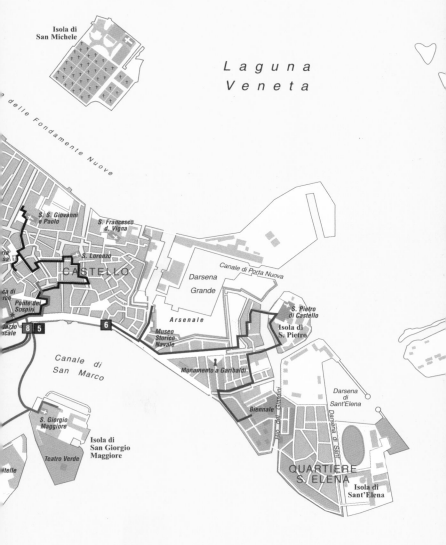

Isola di
Murano

Isola di
San Michele

L a g u n a
V e n e t a

delle Fondamente Nuove

S. S. Giovanni
e Paolo

S. Francesco
d. Vigna

S. Lorenzo

CASTELLO

Canale di Porta Nuova

Darsena
Grande

Ponte dei
Sospiri

Arsenale

S. Pietro
di Castello

ca di
rco

Museo
Storico
Navale

Isola di
S. Pietro

8 5

6

lazzo
ncale

Canale di
San Marco

Monumento a Garibaldi

Darsena
di
Sant'Elena

S. Giorgio
Maggiore

Biennale

Rio dei Giardini

Isola di
San Giorgio
Maggiore

Teatro Verde

Darsena di Sant'

itelle

QUARTIERE
S. ELENA

Isola di
Sant'Elena

INSIGHT GUIDES

VENICE
StepbyStep

Part of the Langenscheidt Publishing Group

CONTENTS

ABOUT THIS BOOK

Above from top: highlights of Venice: Basilica San Marco; Grand Canal; gondoliers; gondolas; pretty backstreets.

This *Step by Step Guide* has been produced by the editors of Insight Guides, whose books have set the standard for visual travel guides since 1970. With top-quality photography and authoritative recommendations, this guidebook brings you the very best of Venice in a series of 14 tailor-made tours.

WALKS AND TOURS

The tours in the book provide something to suit all budgets, tastes and trip lengths. As well as covering Venice's many classic attractions, the routes also track lesser-known sights and up-and-coming areas. The tours embrace a range of interests, so whether you are an animal-lover, an architecture enthusiast, an art fan, a film buff or have kids to entertain, you will find an option to suit.

We strongly recommend that you read the whole of a tour before setting out. This should help you to familiarise yourself with the route and enable you to plan where to stop for refreshments – options for this are given in the blue 'Food and Drink' boxes, which are recog-nisable by the knife-and-fork sign, on most pages.

For our pick of the walks by theme, consult Recommended Tours For… *(see pp.6–7)*.

OVERVIEW

The tours are set in context by this introductory section, giving an overview of the city to set the scene, plus background information on food, drink, shopping and culture. A succinct history timeline in this chapter highlights the key events that have shaped Venice over the centuries.

DIRECTORY

Also supporting the tours is a Directory chapter, comprising a user-friendly, clearly organised A–Z of practical information, our pick of where to stay while you are in the city, nightlife listings and select restaurant recommendations; these eateries complement the more low-key cafés and restaurants that feature within the tours themselves, and are intended to offer a wider choice for evening dining.

The Authors

Jessica Stewart first fell in love with Italy during her high-school years, going on to obtain a degree in art history and study abroad in Padua. Several years ago, after finishing a graduate degree in Renaissance studies, she moved from the US to Rome for career involving the art and culture she is passionate about. As part of her work with the organisation Context Travel, she spends several days a month in Venice exploring its labyrinthine streets and gathering information on food, art, shopping and new trends for savvy travellers.

Many of the tours in this book were originally conceived by Italy specialist Susie Boulton, who has travelled extensively in Italy for over 25 years, and has written and contributed to many of Insight's Italian titles.

Margin Tips
Shopping tips, historical facts, handy hints and information on activities help visitors to make the most of their time in Venice.

Feature Boxes
Notable topics are highlighted in these special boxes.

Key Facts Box
This box gives details of the distance covered on the tour, plus an estimate of how long it should take. It also states where the route starts and finishes, and gives key travel information such as which days are best to do the route or handy transport tips.

Route Map
Detailed cartography shows the itinerary clearly plotted with numbered dots. For more detailed mapping, see the pull-out map slotted inside the back cover.

Footers
Look here for the tour name, a map reference and the main attraction on the double-page.

CULTURE

For most visitors, evening entertainment takes the form of concerts and, especially now that La Fenice has finally reopened, opera. Here we give the low-down on concerts, opera, theatre and film.

CONCERTS AND OPERA

THEATRE

CINEMA

Set in Venice

22 OVERVIEW   ENTERTAINMENT 23

THE SESTIERE OF SAN MARCO

The loop in the Grand Canal enclosed by San Marco is known as 'the seven carps between the bridges', a succession of theatrical spaces, each with inviting bars and monumental palaces.

DISTANCE 3km (2 miles)
TIME A full day
START/END Piazza San Marco
POINTS TO NOTE

Leave **Piazza San Marco**

AROUND LA FENICE

Campo San Fantin

Campo Santa Maria del Giglio

Food and Drink

46 THE SESTIERE OF SAN MARCO   LA FENICE 47

Food and Drink
Recommendations of where to stop for refreshment are given in these boxes. The numbers prior to each restaurant/café name link to references in the main text. Restaurants in the Food and Drink boxes are plotted on the maps.

The € signs at the end of each entry reflect the approximate cost of a two-course meal for one, with a glass of house wine. These should be seen as a guide only. Price ranges, also quoted on the inside back flap for easy reference, are:

€€€€	60 euros and above
€€€	40–60 euros
€€	25–40 euros
€	25 euros and below

ARCHITECTURE FANS

City highlights include St Mark's unrestrainedly decorative basilica (walk 1), Venetian Gothic palaces, such as the Ca' d'Oro, on the Grand Canal (tour 2), classical Venetian grandeur at the Gesuati (walk 7), the Palladian masterpieces of San Giorgio Maggiore and Il Redentore (tour 8) and the magnificent Gothic church of the Frari (walk 9).

RECOMMENDED TOURS FOR...

ART BUFFS

While away a few hours in Accademia (tour 3), visit the Peggy Guggenheim Collection in Dorsoduro (walk 7) or marvel at the works of Tintoretto, Titian and Bellini on the art-packed walk 9. The Querini-Stampalia (walk 5) is also a lovely little gallery of Venetian paintings.

CHILDREN

Head up the bell tower in Piazza San Marco (walk 1) for great views, take a boat trip on the Grand Canal (tour 2), sample the mouth-watering ice creams at the Zattere (tour 7) or have fun on the beach at the Lido (tour 13).

ESCAPING THE CROWDS

It may be jam-packed around Piazza San Marco, but just off the beaten track, in areas such as Castello (walk 5) and Cannaregio (walk 11), you should be able to find peace and quiet – or at least mix with more locals than tourists; for real tranquillity, visit the cemetery island of San Michele (tour 11).

FILM FANS

Admire the Grand Canal palaces (tour 2) that featured in *Casino Royale*, pay homage to Visconti's *Death in Venice* at the Lido's Hôtel des Bains (tour 13) and visit Castello (walks 5 and 6) and San Polo (walk 9), where parts of *Don't Look Now* were screened.

FOODIES

Foodies are well advised to head off the beaten track to discover authentic Venetian bars and restaurants. Try Cannaregio (walk 11) for traditional *bacari*, the Rialto (walk 10) for authentic old bars and around the quiet squares and backstreets in Castello, San Polo or Dorsoduro for funkier, reinvented *bacari* (walks 5, 6, 7 and 9).

LITERATURE BUFFS

Marcel Proust pondered the passing of time at the Caffè Florian (walk 1), Lord Byron occupied several palaces on the Grand Canal (tour 2) and Ernest Hemingway was a regular at Harry's Bar (walk 4). For home-grown writers, visit the Casa Goldoni (walk 9), birthplace of the 18th-century Venetian playwright.

MUSIC-LOVERS

After twice being reduced to ashes by fire, La Fenice has been restored and can be visited on tours; pass it on walk 4. Otherwise, look out for classical concerts in the Scuole (walk 9), in churches such as the La Salute (tour 7), the Frari (walk 9), Santa Maria Formosa (walk 5) and La Pietà (*see p.22*), and palaces including the Ca' Rezzonico (tour 2) and the Querini-Stampalia (walk 5).

RAINY DAYS

Postpone your gondola ride for another day, and pass the time instead under cover in art galleries such as the Accademia (tour 3) or the Peggy Guggenheim Collection (walk 7) or churches from the Basilica di San Marco (walk 1) to La Salute (tour 7).

SHOPPERS

The area west of San Marco (walk 4) is where to buy designer wares, but for typically Venetian items, try Santa Croce (walk 9) for masks and other artisan goods, the Rialto (walk 10) for food, and Murano and Burano (tour 12) for glass and lace respectively.

OVERVIEW

An overview of Venice's geography, customs and culture, plus illuminating background information on food and drink, shopping, carnival, culture and history.

INTRODUCTION

More like a stage set than a city, Venice has captivated visitors for centuries. It dazzles and mesmerises, although it can also overwhelm and confuse the unprepared. It doesn't take long to discover why one of the world's greatest maritime powers has become one of its biggest tourist attractions.

Endlessly portrayed by writers, painters and philosophers, Venice is a canvas for every clichéd fantasy. Almost everyone who is anyone has been there. Even the cafés of Piazza San Marco are awash with famous ghosts. As a result, Venice can play cultural one-upmanship better than most cities. The Romantics were rewarded with a feeling of having come too late to a world too old. The Victorians saw

Below: statue of a Venetian doge.

Venice as dying, while contemporary doom-mongers now seek to bury the city anew. Although entombment by the sea would show symmetry, this resilient city rejects such neat scenarios, with new life and vitality being pumped through its veins.

The only city in the world built entirely on water, Venice is no mere fantasy land, but a superior theme park that can uplift the spirit. You can sleep in Tchaikovsky's bed or wake up in cavernous apartments that once welcomed princes and doges, Henry James and Hemingway. For romance, you can literally walk in Casanova's footsteps; for Baroque passion, succumb to a Vivaldi concerto in Vivaldi's church, or savour the gondoliers' songs that inspired Verdi and Wagner. If you are feeling adventurous, explore the world of Marco Polo in his home city, bargain in the Rialto with latter-day merchants of Venice, or pick up the cobalt-blue cabbages that sent Elizabeth David into culinary raptures.

If you are feeling contemplative, you can ponder the passing of time with Proust's ghost in Caffè Florian. If fortunate, you can capture Canaletto's views with your camera or see Titian's painting in the church it was designed for. If gregarious, you can savour the gossip and

Martinis at Harry's Bar, Hemingway's favourite. The morbid can play roulette in Wagner's death chamber, now the city casino; the melancholic can even die in Thomas Mann's Venice, followed by a costly but atmospheric burial in Stravinsky's cemetery.

For more than a millennium, the Republic of Venice used all its strength to repel unwelcome invaders. Today one of the world's greatest maritime powers has become one of the world's greatest tourist attractions. Its singularity can disorient those who arrive unprepared, but it is this sheer uniqueness that makes it a wonder of the world.

NAVIGATING THE CITY

Venice is traditionally divided into six *sestieri* (districts), all with very different characters. This guide will introduce you to them all, outline a vaporetto (ferry) trip along the Grand Canal and bring you to the islands in the lagoon. As well as encompassing many of the city's architectural glories, this will give you an idea of the layout of the city, including many hidden gems often overlooked by the average visitor. Despite its watery character, you will find that you can get around most of the city on foot, with occasional trips on ferries for circling the city or taking you to the far corners of the lagoon.

Pounding the Streets

Venice is a marvellous city to explore on foot. If you leave behind the crowds of San Marco, you will soon find yourself immersed in a warren of narrow alleys,

back canals and rambling *campi* (squares). Wherever you go there will be cafés where you can linger alfresco, or tiny *bacari* (bars) where you can enjoy a glass of wine and Venetian tapas.

Venetian Addresses

These can be very confusing, labelled by just the street number and neighbourhood: if in doubt, to find an address, ask the name of the closest parish church; this is more helpful than the postal address. Venetians will usually point you in the right direction. Despite the kindness of strangers, all visitors eventually lose themselves in this labyrinthine city. Don't worry, Venetians get lost too, so you are in good company.

The uniqueness of the city geography is captured in Venetian dialect, with the names of streets providing clues to the nature of the city. Familiarity with these terms will help in identifying places on your trails through the confusing backwaters. Venetian spelling is variable, so expect alternative versions. For a list, *see 100*.

NEIGHBOURHOODS

Piazza San Marco is everybody's starting point. The beautifully proportioned square that Napoleon termed 'the finest drawing room in Europe' is the site of the great Basilica, the Doge's Palace and gracious cafés.

Castello

To the north and east of San Marco lies Castello, the largest *sestiere*, offering a slice of everyday life, as dark

Above from far left: St Mark's Basilica in the late-afternoon sun; transport, Venetian-style; painting of a Venetian mask; the oldest bridge in Venice.

Above: lion of St Mark; water marker; view of St Mark's from the island of San Giorgio Maggiore.

alleys open onto bright, bustling squares. The area is home to several major churches, as well as the Arsenale, the great military and naval complex founded in the 12th century, and the Biennale gardens, home to the contemporary art and architecture shows that give Venice a modern edge.

San Polo and Santa Croce
San Polo and Santa Croce are two adjoining districts that encompass the labyrinthine Rialto market, the famous Rialto Bridge that traditionally divided the city and the Frari, the greatest of all Venetian Gothic churches.

Cannaregio and Dorsoduro
Cannaregio is the most densely populated district, but it's home to some lovely churches as well as the former Jewish Ghetto. Dorsoduro is the *sestiere* for some delightful walks along the Zattere quayside, as well as visits to La Salute church, the Accademia and the Peggy Guggenheim collection of modern art. It's also a hub of young life in Venice, being the centre of Ca' Foscari University.

Islands of the Lagoon
For those who have time, there are the islands to explore, easily reached by frequent ferries. Murano is famous for its glass-making, Burano for its lace and its colourful fishermen's cottages, and Torcello for its cathedral, the oldest monument in the lagoon. Giudecca, an island that is undergoing a rebirth, is home to Il Redentore church, a Palladian masterpiece, and the most luxurious hotel in Venice, the Cipriani. San Giorgio Maggiore is the site of a famous Benedictine monastery; while the Lido, a long strip of land between the

city and the Adriatic, glories in its role as a superior film set.

VENICE IN PERIL

Venice officially stopped sinking in 1983. The biggest watery threats now are *acqua alta* (high water) and wave damage from boats to the foundations of buildings. During autumn and winter duckboards are a familiar sight in low-lying Piazza San Marco. Work is going ahead on the hugely controversial Mose project, the mobile flood barriers that will close off the lagoon during the high tides. Environmentalists are trying to halt the project; even those in favour see it merely as a means of buying time.

Meanwhile, rocketing house prices (driven up by foreign buyers) are forcing Venetians out to cheaper accommodation on the mainland. Another serious problem is the influx of private homes renovated into bed-and-breakfast accommodation, leaving little room for families. Since 1966 the population has halved from 121,000 to 61,000. If the exodus continues at the present rate there will be no Venetians left by the mid-21st century.

THE VENETIANS

The character of the city 'is old, conservative and resistant to change. Here in the historic centre we lack the capacity for renewal, or even the numbers required to effect a change'. Massimo Cacciari, the re-elected mayor of Venice, speaks as ponderously and lugubriously as ever. Certainly, the population is ageing, with the number of visitors greatly exceeding that of the resident population.

Yet the elusive Venetian spirit transcends such truisms, defies the simple arithmetic of the doom-mongers, and refuses to be confined by the straitjacket of tourism. In a city defined by the sea, there can be no fortress mentality, only ebb and flow. Cool, independent Venetians are nothing if not survivors.

Cacciari is sanguine about the future of his fellow citizens and beloved city: 'If Venice has any vitality left, it will seize the moment. If it is dead in human terms, it will die. After all, Babylon, Alexandria and Rome have all died.' While at odds with the Venetians' positive approach to life, this view echoes the citizens' classic philosophical detachment. As such, the mayor shows himself to be a contradictory character, and that is the mark of a true Venetian.

Renovation Projects

Bear in mind that there will always be unexpectedly closed sections of galleries and churches in Venice, as ongoing restoration is a feature of the city. Changes in opening times are listed in a free magazine from the tourist office. For details on the civic museums, see www.museicivici veneziani.it. There are several non-profit organisations dedicated to the upkeep and renovation of Venetian monuments, notably Venice in Peril (www.veniceinperil. org), created by the British Ambassador to Italy after the floods of 1966.

Booking and Discounts

Hello Venezia (tel: 041-2424; www.hellovenezia.it; 7.30am–8pm) is the place to book opera, concerts, ballet and events. It also sells the useful Venice Card, a discounted combined ticket allowing access to all the museums on San Marco, including the Museo Correr, plus unlimited use of public transport, access to all Chorus Churches and reductions at many other sites. The card can be purchased for 3 days or 7 days. Chorus Churches, comprising 16 of the city's best religious buildings, sells a pass that offers free entry for one year (tel: 041-275 0462; www.chorusvenezia.org). Venezia Si is an organisation representing over 90 percent of Venetian hoteliers, but it also accepts bookings for major exhibitions and concerts (from abroad call: +39 041-522 2264; in Italy call: 199-173 309; www.veneziasi.it).

FOOD AND DRINK

Venice is noted for top-quality seafood and for fine restaurants. But you shouldn't ignore the traditional bars and inns, known as bacari. This is where you will find more locals and will be able to taste a number of traditional foodstuffs at a reasonable cost.

Booking Ahead
Reservations are essential, especially at weekends, at any restaurant in Venice. As the highest-quality eateries are coveted by Venetians and travellers alike (and the interior spaces small), you will want to call a day or so in advance to assure yourself a table. Also, remember most restaurants close between lunch and dinner, so it's advisable to have lunch between noon and 1pm. If you are hungry between these times, pop into a bar for some *tramezzini* (little triangular sandwiches on white bread).

Food critics tend to damn Venetian food as overpriced and under-achieving, but you can eat well if you choose wisely. Even so, the difficulty of transporting fresh produce generally adds 20 percent to restaurant prices. Mass tourism also means that the city can get away with grim tourist menus, indifferent service and inferior break-fasts. This also means one must keep an eye on quality, for what was a hidden treasure one day can quickly become a low-quality eatery after gaining popularity. Yet for seafood-lovers, the cuisine can be memorable, with soft-shelled crabs from the lagoon, plump red mullet, pasta heaped with lobster or black and pungent with cuttlefish ink.

VENETIAN CUISINE

According to top British chef and Italophile Alastair Little, 'The city's cosmopolitan past and superb produce imported from the Veneto have given rise to Italy's most eclectic and subtle style of cookery.' Like the Sicilians, the Venetians absorbed culinary ideas from the Arabs; they also raided Byzantium and, according to the Middle Eastern cookery writer Claudia Roden, translated it into their own simple style: 'If you could see the fish come in live at dawn in barges on the Grand Canal straight onto the market stalls, you would understand why all they want to do is lightly fry, poach or grill it.'

Culinary Melting Pot

As the hub of a cosmopolitan trading empire, Venice was bristling with foreign communities – Arabs, Armenians, Greeks, Jews and Turks – each with its own culinary tradition. Venetian trading posts in the Levant gave the city access to spices, the secret of subtle Venetian cookery. Pimiento, turmeric, ginger, cinnamon, cumin, cloves, nutmeg, saffron and vanilla show the oriental influences; pine-nuts, raisins, almonds and pistachios also play their part.

Reflecting later conquests of Venice, these exotic ingredients are enriched with a dash of French or Austrian cuisine. From the end of the 18th century, French influence meant that oriental spices were supplanted by Mediter-ranean herbs. The French brioche was added to the breakfast repertoire, as was the Turkish *crescente* (literally a crescent). The appearance of the crois-sant dates back to the Turkish defeat at the walls of Vienna in 1683. The Aus-

trian conquest may have left Venice with a bitter taste in its mouth, but it also left the city with an appetite for apple strudel and *krapfen* (doughnuts).

Eclectic Tastes

A classic Middle Eastern-inspired dish is *sarde in saor*, tart sardines marinated in standard Venetian sauce. *Melanzane in saor*, made with aubergines, is the vegetarian version. *Saor* means savoury or tasty, and is a spicy sauce made with permutations of onions, raisins, vinegar, pine-nuts and olive oil. *Riso* (rice), rather than pasta, predominates, prized for its versatility ever since its introduction by the Arabs. Creamy Venetian risotto offers endless possibilities, flavoured with spring vegetables, meat, game or fish. *Risi e bisi* (rice and peas) is a thick soup blended with ham, celery and onion. Equally delicious are the seasonal risottos, cooked with asparagus tips, artichoke hearts, fennel, courgettes or pumpkins. An oriental variant involves sultanas and pine-nuts.

Fish Dishes

Given the European climate of health scares, some visitors avoid the lagoon fish, fearing mercury contamination. However, the fish on most local menus come from the Adriatic. Inland fishing also occurs in *valli*, fenced-off sections of the lagoon, mainly for grey mullet (*cefalu*) and eel (*anguilla*). It is hard to better *antipasti di frutti di mare*, a feast of simply cooked shellfish and molluscs, dressed with olive oil and lemon juice; prawns and soft-shelled

crabs vie with baby octopus and squid. A trademark dish is cuttlefish risotto, served black and pungent with ink, or *granseola*, spider crab, boiled and then dressed simply in lemon and oil. Another staple is *baccalà*, dried salt cod, prepared with milk and herbs or parmesan and parsley, and served in countless ways, including on toasted bread. In Venice, fish features more often than meat, but offal is favoured, particularly in *fegato alla veneziana*, calf's liver sliced into ribbons and cooked with parsley and onion.

DESSERTS

Save room for pudding, because Venetian biscuits, cakes and desserts are excellent, flavoured with exotic

Cichetti

Some of the most common *cichetti* (Venetian tapas) are *polpette* (spicy meatballs), *carciofini* (artichoke hearts), crostini with grilled vegetables, *baccalà mantecato* (salted cod on polenta), *seppie roste* (grilled cuttlefish) and anchovy nibbles. Keep track of what you eat, as you'll be charged per piece (prices start from €1).

Above: fresh produce at market at the Rialto.

spices since the discovery of cinnamon and nutmeg. The Venetians introduced cane sugar to Europe, and have retained their sweet tooth. Spicy sweets are popular, including *fritelle di zucca*, sweet pumpkin doughnut served hot, while the best ices can be found in *gelaterie* on the Zattere.

WHERE TO EAT

In terms of where to eat, San Marco and Castello are home to some of the city's most prestigious restaurants, but privacy is rare in these goldfish-bowl settings. Further away from the bustle, dining experiences tend to be more varied, and prices lower. Try Cannaregio and Dorsoduro for the best variety of high-quality, well-priced meals. Not that visitors should ignore overtly glamorous spots; the Venetians patronise them too. But beyond St Mark's, a number of ethnic restaurants have opened, and late-night dining has become far more widespread, although in most places you are advised not to arrive for dinner much after 8.30pm.

Styles of Restaurant

In style, Venetian restaurants seem to opt for cool, 18th-century elegance, or the exposed beams and copper pots that spell rustic gentility. Yet individualistic inns abound, whether tucked under pergolas or spilling onto terraces and courtyards. Reservations are required for the grander restaurants, which tend to be fairly dressy affairs, reflecting the elegant setting. The opposite is true of the *bacari*, the trad-

itional wine bars, where you can dress as a market trader if you feel like it.

More upmarket places are termed *ristoranti*, but may be called *osterie* (inns) if they focus on homely food in an intimate or rustic setting. To confuse the issue, some inns have bars that act like traditional *bacari*, so that one can opt for a quicker, cheaper snack at the bar or a full sit-down meal at a table.

The distinction between bars and restaurants is somewhat confused in Venice, as most *bacari* also serve food, typically the Venetian equivalent of tapas, known as *cichetti*. To eat *cichetti e l'ombra*, a snack and a glass of wine, is a Venetian tradition.

DRINKS

Wine

The Veneto produces a number of superior (DOC) wines, from the fruity, garnet-red Bardolino to the less prestigious Valpolicella. Venetians drink much more white wine, partly through habit, partly because it accompanies seafood better. Soave is the Veneto's best-known but rather bland white; it comes from vineyards dotted along the eastern shores of Lake Garda. Dry whites from the Veneto and Friuli, such as Soave or Pinot Grigio, are recommended accompaniments to seafood dishes.

Cocktails

Venice is noted for its cocktails, especially the Bellini, a peach-and-prosecco aperitif created in Harry's Bar. Prosecco, the sparkling wine from the Veneto,

makes a fine aperitif, whether drunk dry *(secco)* or medium sweet *(amabile)*. As such, it is Italian champagne, yet drunk at the drop of a hat.

But to look like a Venetian, risk the lurid orange cocktail known as spritz (pronounced 'spriss' in Venetian dialect). The bright-orange drink was introduced under Austrian rule (named after the introduction of 'selzer', fizzy soda water) and soon became a firm favourite. It consists of roughly equal parts of dry white wine, soda water and an aperitif, usually Campari or Aperol, and garnished with a twist of lemon or an olive. Ask for a *spritz al bitter* for a stronger, less cloying taste. The spritz may be an acquired taste, but once acquired, it's the clearest sign that you've fallen for Venice.

Where to Drink

Not much changes in the historic cafés close to San Marco, where coffee has been drunk for centuries and post-prandial grappas downed since the days of the doges. Yet just beyond San Marco are serious wine bars *(enoteche)*, where tastings are the main draw. Over the last few years, there has been a trend for new wine bars, too, including cool reinterpretations of the *bacaro*; some are sleek new designer gastro-bars that would be at home in Manhattan – apart, of course, for the gondola moored by the back door. Even a number of once-staid hotel cocktail bars have been successfully relaunched as cool lounge bars. As a result, Venetian bar culture is far broader than time-warp piano bars in sophisticated hotels.

Above from far left: neighbourhood café in Dorsoduro; Vino Vino (see p.47), in San Marco.

Cocktail Hour
Between 7pm and 8pm is 'cocktail hour', a Venetian ritual. At this time, the locals can be seen sipping wine or classic cocktails in both chic cafés and old-fashioned neighbourhood bars or *bacari*.

Below: coffee served in splendour on Piazzetta San Marco.

SHOPPING

To enjoy the excitement of finding something truly Venetian, you need curiosity, conviction and a substantial budget. Focus on arts and crafts, especially luxury fabrics, glassware, marbled paper and Venetian masks.

Above: Murano glass door knobs.

Opening Hours
Many stores keep opening hours of 9:30/10am to 12.30/1pm and then 3.30/4pm until 7.30/8pm, so plan your shopping accordingly. Many smaller boutiques also close for the day on either Sunday or Monday. Some stores close either in August for the summer vacation or in January, when fewer visitors are in the city. Larger shops and department stores, especially near San Marco, tend, however, to stay open all day.

MASKS AND COSTUMES

If you want to buy a Venetian mask, always check what it is made of and ask the seller to tell you how it fits into the Venetian tradition – whether it is a character from the *commedia dell'arte (see p.69)*, for example. For women, the Civetta is a flirtatious, catlike mask, while the Colombina is more ladylike. One of the most appealing mask shops lies in the Castello district, in the quiet canals behind San Zaccaria, Ca' del Sol (Castello 4964, Fondamenta del Osmarin; tel: 041-528 5549). Mondonovo is one of the most creative mask-makers (Dorsoduro 3063; Rio Terrà Canal, off Campo Santa Margherita; tel: 041-528 7344). Also in Dorsoduro, Ca' Macana (Dorsoduro 3172, Calle della Botteghe; tel: 041-277 6142), offers mask-making courses. Flavia (Corte Specchiera, Castello; tel: 041-528 7429) hires or sells carnival costumes.

TEXTILES

Venice is well known for its Fortuny fabrics – silks and velvets, plain or gloriously patterned. Venetia Studium (San Marco 2403, Calle Larga XXII Marzo; tel: 041-522 9281) produces exclusive fabrics, including Fortuny designs, from scarves to cushion covers to lamps, as well as delicately patterned fabrics and soft furnishings. Another big name in Venetian fabrics is Bevilacqua (San Marco 337b, Ponte della Canonica; tel: 041-528 7581; also at San Marco 2520; tel: 041-241 0662), which has been producing Venetian velvets and brocades since 1875; many are still produced on traditional 18th-century wooden looms.

Jesurum (Cannaregio 3219, Fondamenta della Sensa; tel: 041-524 2540) has been selling princely household linen, including embroidered sheets, since 1870. Frette (San Marco 2070a, Calle Larga XXII Marzo; tel: 041-522 4914) sells fine linens, exquisite sheets, cushions and bathrobes.

MARBLED PAPER

Between San Marco and the Rialto are shops selling marbled paper. Called *legatoria* or 'book-binding', this ancient craft gives paper a decorative marbled veneer and is used nowadays for photo albums, writing cases, greeting cards, diaries and notebooks. Good stockists include Paoli Olbi (Cannaregio 6061, Campo Santa Maria Nova; tel: 041-523 7655) and Cartavenezia (Santa Croce 2125, Calle Longa; tel: 041-524 1283).

MURANO GLASS

Only buy glass guaranteed by the Vetro Artistico Murano trademark (www.muranoglass.com). Remember that Murano glass can be found both on the island itself but also in numerous ateliers in the lagoon. Also, resist the hard sell before you know what you like.

One of the most prestigious contemporary glassmakers is Venini (shop on Piazzetta Leoncini, San Marco 314, with factory and showrooms on Fondamenta Vetrai 50, Murano; tel: 041-273 7211). Barovier e Toso (Murano, Fondamenta Vetrai 28; tel: 041-527 4385) is equally respected and is in simpler taste than many others. Paul & C (San Marco 4391a, Calle Larga San Marco; tel: 041-520 9899) is for serious shoppers, with sales direct from the Murano factories. Archimede Seguso is a prestigious firm, with a shop on Piazza San Marco (no. 143; tel: 041-528 9041). In the lagoon, try smaller ateliers such as Giorgio Nason (Dorsoduro 167, Campo San Gregorio; tel: 041-523 9426) for jewellery or Vittorio Costantini (Cannaregio 5311, Calle del Fumo; tel: 041-522 2265) for small glass animals, including insects.

BOOKS AND PRINTS

Bookworms should head for Mondadori (San Marco 1345, Salizzada San Moise), a cool, central late-night bookshop, gallery and multimedia centre with Bacaro, an equally hip bar, attached. Other shops include Libreria Sansovino (San Marco 84, Bacina

Orseolo), which specialises in books on Venice, and Old World Books (Cannaregio 1190, Ponte del Ghetto Vecchio), which stocks rare or out-of-print books.

For prints, La Stamperia del Ghetto (Cannaregio 1185a, Calle del Ghetto Vecchio; tel: 041-275 0200) includes general and Jewish themes. Gianni Basso (Cannaregio 5306, Calle del Fumo; tel: 041-523 4681) churns out business cards, bookplates and stationery for worldwide clients in his tiny printing studio.

DESIGNER GOODS

The full range of Italian designer goods are on sale in Venice, but prices tend to be higher than on the mainland. The most elegant designer boutiques are on Calle Vallaresso, Salizzada San Moisè, the Frezzeria and Calle Larga XXII Marzo, west of San Marco. The classic fabric and haberdashery quarter is the Mercerie, a maze of alleys sandwiched between San Marco and the Rialto. More everyday shops lie between Campo San Salvador and Santo Stefano and in the Castello district, while the Rialto fish-and-vegetable market is the most intoxicating place for foodstuffs. The Rialto shopping alleys are also lively in the early evening, with Ruga Vecchia di San Giovanni home to good food shops. If you hanker after copies of designer bags and belts, fake Louis Vuitton or Gucci, the African traders will catch your attention around Calle Larga XXII Marzo or on bustling Riva degli Schiavoni.

Above from far left: Venetian mask; Burano lace parasols; glassware for sale at a market stall in Cannaregio.

Hip Dorsoduro Head to Dorsoduro for some of the most trendy and artistic boutiques in the city. As many artists live in the area, this *sestiere* is bursting with contemporary art galleries, printmakers and designers.

Department Stores Coin (Salizzada San Giovanni Crisostomo) is one of the few department stores in Venice.

CARNIVAL

Every year in the run-up to Shrove Tuesday, the city indulges in a 10-day masked ball – a Lententide 'farewell to the flesh' – as La Serenissima awakes to a whirl of colour, masks and costumes, each year with a different theme.

Buying a Mask

If you want to buy a mask, it is worth visiting one of the traditional made-to-measure mask shops, where they can whip you up anything from a brightly coloured festive Harlequin to a Medusa wreathed in snakes. The most traditional masks are made of leather *(in cuoio)* or papier mâché *(in cartapesta)*, with modern creations worked in ceramics or covered with luxurious fabrics. Leather masks are the hardest to fashion, while hand-held masks make striking wall decorations. (If you want inspiration for historically authentic carnival costumes, study Pietro Longhi's exquisite carnival paintings, in the Ca' Rezzonico; see p.39.)

Above from left:

white masks; glamorous carnival mask; covering the face enabled the social classes to mix without anyone realising it.

The Venetian carnival is the inheritor of a rich folk tradition, embracing pagan and Christian motifs. Linked to the winter solstice and fertility rites, such midwinter folk festivals predate Christianity. According to pagan rites, winter was a force to be overcome, with the sun persuaded to return by a show of life at its most vital.

Christianity gave the carnival new significance: the words *carne vale*, the Latin for 'farewell to meat', meant a last blow-out, particularly on Mardi Gras (Fat Tuesday), before the start of the long and rigorous Lenten period, marked by abstinence from the pleasures of the flesh and a focus on the spiritual.

In the past, the Venetian carnival was something of a movable feast, beginning as early as October or Christmas and lasting until Lent. This long carnival season incorporated an element of 'bread and circuses', with crowd-pleasing performances intended to curry favour with the populace. In addition to masquerades, there were rope dancers, acrobats and fire-eaters who routinely displayed their skills on Piazza San Marco. The diarist John Evelyn visited Venice in 1645–6 and reported on 'the folly and madness of the carnival', from the bull-baiting and flinging of eggs to the superb opera, the singing eunuch and a shooting

incident with an enraged nobleman and his courtesan, whose gondola canoodling he had disturbed. During the 1751 carnival, everyone gathered to admire an exotic beast, the rhinoceros, captured in a famous painting by Longhi, which is now displayed in the Ca' Rezzonico *(see p.39)*.

When Napoleon conquered Venice in 1797, the carnival went the tragic way of the Venetian Republic. Although revived sporadically in the early part of the 20th century, it was only fully restored in 1979. The event was eagerly reclaimed by Venetians, with playful processions and masquerades.

It is fashionable to mock the carnival as a commercial fabrication, but its roots extend deep into the Venetian psyche. The city has an instinctive love of spectacle and dressing up, dating back to the glory days of the Republic. The carnival reaches back to medieval times and represents a cavalcade of Venetian history, tracing political and military events, factional rivalries and defeats.

FESTIVE CALENDAR

Thousands of masqueraders see in the carnival on Piazza San Marco. This event is followed by pantomime, operetta, concerts and literary readings in theatres and alfresco in the city's

campi. Campo San Polo, one of the largest squares, is a popular site for outdoor events, thus maintaining a role it has played here since medieval times. Many of the finest masked balls, fireworks and historical happenings are led by the Compagnie della Calza, the local carnival companies.

The high point of the festival is on Shrove Tuesday, when revellers gather for a masked ball on Piazza San Marco before moving on to private parties or, in the case of celebrities, to the ball at the Cipriani, across the water. In the past, the midnight fasting bell would ring out from San Francesco della Vigna, signalling an end to licence and the onset of atonement. The end is signalled when the effigy of Carnival is burnt on Piazza San Marco.

CARNIVAL MASKS

Venetian carnival masks seem timeless. In fact, the most traditional masks form a dramatic monochrome disguise, often harking back to periods of Venetian history or the dramatic tradition of the *commedia dell'arte (see p.69)*. Masks not based on traditional designs are generally known as *fantasie*, or fantasy masks. One of the very finest is the *maschera nobile*, the white sculpted mask, with a black tricorn hat and black silk cloak. Columbina (Columbine) is the name given to the elegant Venetian domino mask; more catlike and seductive is the mask commonly called *civetta* (flirt). Some masks are quite sinister, notably the menacing Plague Doctor, which features a distinctive beaked nose and

black gown and was once worn as a protection against the plague.

CARNIVAL TODAY

Carnival has much to answer for: prices soar, and the city has more mask shops than butchers; fashion shoots and foreign film crews swamp San Marco; cavorting crowds of motley Europeans dress as gondoliers and bosomy courtesans. Yet despite the commercialism, this kitsch masquerade retains its magic.

Today's carnival plays homage to the lavish lifestyles of 18th-century Venice. Costumes currently in vogue extol the voluptuous femininity of 18th-century dress for both sexes. The classic costume of the 17th and 18th centuries was the *maschera nobile*, the patrician mask. The head was covered with a *bautá*, a black silk hood and lace cape, topped by a voluminous cloak *(tabarro)*, in black silk for the nobility and in red or grey for ordinary citizens. The *volto*, the white half-mask, covered the face, with the finishing touch provided by a black tricorn hat adorned with feathers.

The elegant *maschera nobile* and *commedia dell'arte* masks are not the only authentic disguises. Masks representing or ridiculing the Republic's enemies, such as a Moor or Turk, remain popular, as do esoteric costumes associated with the carnival companies. Certainly, the Venetian love of disguise masks a desire to slip into a different skin. As Oscar Wilde said, 'A man only reveals himself when wearing a mask.'

Festivals

Chances are there will be some celebration during your stay, since Venice is busy with festivals and events all year round. The city plays host to water festivals redolent of the pomp and pageantry of the Republic, the grandest of which is the Historic Regatta, dating from 1825 and held on the first Sunday in September. The calvacade of boats winds its way from the Giardini quarter to Ca' Foscari on the Grand Canal, where prizes are presented from dignitaries gathered on a decorated barge. It is followed by a gondola race. Other festivities include the Feast of the Redeemer *(see p.64)*; festivities for the city's patron saint, St Mark (25 April); the Film Festival *(see p.23 and p.87)*; the Art Biennale and Architecture Biennale (held in September on subsequent years); and the November Festival Musica Internazionale, which focuses on chamber music, Baroque works, ballroom dancing, piano recitals, jazz, big-band music and even Spanish guitar.

CULTURE

For most visitors, evening entertainment takes the form of concerts and, especially now that La Fenice has finally reopened, opera. Here we give the low-down on concerts, opera, theatre and film.

CONCERTS AND OPERA

Listings Information
To find out what's on, the best sources of information are the tourist office's calendar of opening times, shows, and events, which is free of charge, and the invaluable free booklet, *A Guest in Venice*, available from some hotels (mostly the grand ones) or online at www. unospitedivenezia.it. For upcoming events, see also www.turismo venezia.it and www. culturaspettacolo venezia.it. For a contemporary guide to Venice, try *Venezia da Vivere*, www. veneziadavivere.com (in Italian and English), dedicated to listing information on art openings, concerts and the newest hot spots.

Above from far left: musician in the Piazza San Marco; look out for posters advertising concerts and theatre.

Venetians are passionate about their classical music and proud of the fact that Vivaldi, Monteverdi and Wagner all lived in Venice. Autumn spells the start of the classical music season, and – in November – the start of the opera season at the finally reopened La Fenice (Campo San Fantin, San Marco; tel: 041-786 511; www.teatrolafenice. it; *see p.47*). Performances are also sometimes held at Teatro Malibran (Campiello Malibran, Cannaregio; tel: 041-786 601), which was used as the main theatre while La Fenice was under reconstruction. Concerts are often held in beautiful settings, such as churches, oratories and the *scuole* (charitable confraternity seats, *see below*).

Confraternity Concerts
The Scuola Grande di San Teodoro (tel: 041-521 0294; www.imusiciveneziani. it) stages concerts in the confraternity house, with the singers and orchestra dressed in 18th-century costume. Concerts are also held in the sumptuously decorated confraternity houses of the Scuola Grande di San Rocco (tel: 041-523 4864; *see p.65*), the Scuola Grande dei Carmini (tel: 041-099 4371), the Scuola Grande di San Giovanni Evangelista and the Ospedaletto. Many of

the best concerts are conducted by the Accademia di San Rocco, a musical ensemble that stages Baroque recitals in traditional Venetian settings.

Church Concerts
One of the most popular concert churches is La Pietà (Riva degli Schiavoni), the lovely Rococo church linked to Vivaldi. La Pietà is both a magnificent setting for the Venetian composer's work (Vivaldi's concerts are very popular in Venice) and for concerts of Baroque music.

Classical concerts are also held in the Gothic church of I Frari *(see p.66)*, in Tintoretto's church of Madonna dell'Orto *(see p.77)* and in La Salute *(see p.58)*. The Renaissance church of Santa Maria dei Miracoli *(see p.78)*, the Rialto market church of San Giacometto (tel: 041-426 6559; www.ensemble antonio vivaldi.com) and the neighbourhood Santa Maria Formosa *(see p.52)* are also evocative settings for concerts. On Piazza San Marco, the Ateneo di San Basso (tel: 041-528 2825; www.virtuoso divenezia.com) is the setting for concerts of works by Vivaldi and Mozart.

Palaces
Concerts are also staged in the city's greatest palaces, from Ca' Vendramin-Calergi (usually Wagner) to Ca' Rez-

zonico (generally 18th-century music; *see p.39*). The Fondazione Querini-Stampalia (tel: 041-271 1411; www.querinistempalia.it; *see p.52*) is a small gallery providing an intimate yet sumptuous setting for concerts every Friday and Saturday at 5pm and 7pm.

Outdoor Concerts and Opera

In summer, key squares in the Dorsoduro district are turned into open-air concert venues, including Campo Pisani, just off Campo Santo Stefano. The 1,500-seat Teatro Verde (tel: 900-800 800; www.teatroverde.de) on the island of San Giorgio Maggiore also makes a spectacular setting for opera.

THEATRE

Plays are performed exclusively in Italian in Venice, making a trip feasible only if your language skills are above a certain level. The loveliest theatre is the Teatro Goldoni (Calle Teatro Goldoni, San Marco; tel: 041-240 2011; www.teatrostabileveneto.it), which stages plays by the esteemed Venetian dramatist after whom it is named (Carlo Goldoni, 1707–93). Concerts are also held at the Goldoni.

CINEMA

With the exception of films shown at the festival, most foreign films shown in Italy are dubbed into Italian. *Versione originale* (original version) or *VO* on posters or in listings indicates that films are presented in their original language. Key cinemas include the small Accademia (041-528 7706) in Dorsoduro and (currently closed for renovation) the Rossini in San Marco. Cannaregio's Giorgione Movie d'Essai usually shows foreign films in their original language. (Take vaporetto line no. 1 to the Ca' d'Oro stop to reach it.)

During the glitzy Venice Film Festival *(see right and p.87)*, held in late August and early September, films are shown in their original versions. Venice is the oldest film festival in the world, and second in prestige only to Cannes. Today the festival concentrates on art-house movies rather than blockbusters.

Venice Film Festival
Venice is the home of the world's oldest film festival, founded by Mussolini in 1932. For 10 days in late August/early September the city plays host to a huge cast of Hollywood and European stars, and the attendant paparazzi. The festival is centred on Lido, on the Palazzo del Cinemà, built in the 1930s in triumphant Fascist style. To spot the celebrities, stroll along the beachside boulevard or splash out on a cocktail at the sea-view terrace of the Hotel Excelsior. The Hotel Cipriani *(see p.115)* is also a favourite place to stay for the Hollywood set. Most tickets go to the film and press industries, but some tickets are available to the general public: see www.labiennale.org.

Set in Venice

Venice does not have a film industry but it has been the backdrop of a number of well-known films. These include Michael Radford's 2004 version of Shakespeare's *The Merchant of Venice*, with Al Pacino as Shylock, Nicolas Roeg's 1973 *Don't Look Now*, starring Julie Christie and Donald Sutherland, and Luchino Visconti's 1971 *Death in Venice*, based on Thomas Mann's 1912 novella and starring Dirk Bogarde as Gustav von Aschenbach, who falls in love with a Polish boy while staying at the Lido's Hôtel des Bains. In addition, some scenes from *The Talented Mr Ripley*, Anthony Minghella's adaptation of the Patricia Highsmith novel concerning assumed identity, were set in Venice; also, the well-travelled Mr Bond pops up briefly in *From Russia with Love* (1963), drives a gondola on land in *Moonraker* (1979) and has all kinds of Venetian adventures in the 2006 version of *Casino Royale*.

HISTORY: KEY DATES

From foundation among stagnant marshes on the shores of the Adriatic to glory days as the most powerful city in the West. Thereafter came occupation, flooding, the enduring threat of sinking and a tourism boom.

FIRST SETTLEMENTS

421	Foundation of Venice on 25 March, Feast Day of St Mark.
452–568	Attila the Hun plunders the Veneto. Mass migrations take place from the mainland to Venice.
697	The first doge, Paolo Lucio Anafesto, is elected to office.
814	The population moves to the Rivo Alto (Rialto), a more hospitable and easily defended island. Venetian coins first minted. Work begins on the first Doge's Palace.

HEIGHT OF THE REPUBLIC

Marriage of the Sea
La Sensa, the Ascension festival, celebrates Venice's Marriage with the Sea; this historic festival has been in place since 1000. Until the fall of the Republic, the doge would sail from San Marco to the Lido in the Bucintoro, the ceremonial state barge. With great pomp, a ring was cast into the Adriatic, symbolising Venice's sacred union with the sea. Today's re-enactment is a pale imitation; the water marathon that follows is more memorable: La Vogalonga (Long Row) races from St Mark's Basin to Burano before returning via the Grand Canal.

828	St Mark's body is taken from Alexandria to Venice.
1000	Venice controls the Adriatic coast. The Marriage to the Sea ceremony *(see margin left)* is inaugurated.
1095–9	Venice joins the Crusades, providing ships and supplies for First Crusade to liberate the Holy Land.
1173	First Rialto Bridge begun.
1202–4	Fourth Crusade; the sack of Constantinople and Venetian conquest of Byzantium provide a springboard for the growth of the Venetian empire. Arsenale shipyards are created. Venice becomes a world power.
1309–10	Work begins on the present Doge's Palace. The Council of Ten is established as a check on individual power and a monitor of security.
1348–9	A plague outbreak kills half the people of Venice.
1453–4	Constantinople falls to the Turks; zenith of Venetian empire: Treviso, Bergamo, Ravenna, Friuli, Udine and Istria are all conquered.
1489	Cyprus is ceded to Venice by Queen Caterina Cornaro.
1508	League of Cambrai unites Europe against Venice. Titian's *Assumption* is hung in the Frari church, Venice. Birth of the architect Andrea Palladio in the Veneto.
1571	Battle of Lepanto, a decisive naval victory against the Turks.
1577	Palladio designs Il Redentore church.
1669	Loss of Crete, the last major Venetian colony, to the Turks.
1708	A harsh winter freezes the lagoon; Venetians can walk to the mainland.

1718	Venice surrenders Morea (Peloponnese) to the Turks, signalling the loss of its maritime empire; it is left with the Ionian islands and the Dalmatian coast.
1752	Completion of the sea walls.
1790	Opening of La Fenice opera house.

UNDER OCCUPATION

1797	Fall of the 1,000-year-old Venetian Republic. Doge Lodovico Manin abdicates. Napoleon grants Venice to Austria in return for Lombardy.
1800	Papal conclave in Venice to elect a pope.
1805–14	Napoleonic rule reinstated.
1815–66	Under the terms of the Congress of Vienna, Austria occupies the city.
1846	Venice is joined to the mainland by a railway causeway.
1861	Vittorio Emanuele is crowned king of a united Italy.
1866	Venice is annexed to the Kingdom of Italy.

20TH CENTURY

1931	A road causeway connects city to mainland.
1932	First Venice Film Festival takes place.
1945	British troops liberate city from Nazi occupiers.
1960	Construction of the Marco Polo airport.
1966	The worst flood in Venetian history hits the city.
1979	The Venice Carnival is revived.
1988	First stage of the flood barrier is completed.
1996	Burning down of La Fenice opera house. The worst floods and *acqua alta* (high tides) since 1966.

21ST CENTURY

2003	The Mose (Moses) project gets the go-ahead, and work begins on the new mobile flood barrier, due for completion in 2011.
2004	La Fenice finally reopens after reconstruction, with *La Traviata*. Venice gets broadband via fibre-optic cables, dispensing with the need for ugly satellite dishes.
2008	After several years of delay, the Ponte Calatrava is constructed across the Grand Canal, linking the railway station with Piazzale Roma. Changes abound on the vaporetto, with the introduction of iMod, an electronic, rechargeable ticket, the renumbering of popular line 82 to line 2, and the creation of a 'resident only' vaporetto (line 3).

WALKS AND TOURS

PIAZZA SAN MARCO

Piazza San Marco is the focus of Venetian life. Start with the splendours of the Basilica and the Doge's Palace, then saunter along the Riva degli Schiavoni, relax in a café and absorb the sublime views across the lagoon.

DISTANCE 1km (⅔ mile)
TIME A full day
START Basilica San Marco
END Torre dell' Orologio
POINTS TO NOTE

Booking a slot online at least two days before your visit means that you won't have to join a queue; contact ALATA on www.alata.it (no charge). Another way to avoid queuing is to check in a bag (no large bags or backpacks are allowed inside) at the Ateneo S. Basso (Calle S. Basso, by the Piazzetta dei Leoncini). You will be given a tag that can be taken to the guards and will allow you to skip the queue. To get the best views of the mosaics, visit when the Basilica is illuminated, from 11.30am–12.30pm daily. To avoid the crowds, go early morning or late afternoon, avoiding weekends if possible. Beware that visitors are usually herded through the Basilica and encouraged to spend no more than 10 minutes during a visit. Scantily dressed visitors, eg those wearing shorts or with uncovered shoulders, will be turned away. Expect to see some part of the exterior shrouded in scaffolding and faux murals – viewing the building in its entirety is a rare event.

Acqua Alta

Deadly flooding known as *acqua alta* (high water) invades the low-lying piazza some 250 times a year. The building of a controversial new tidal barrier named MOSE (after the prophet Moses, who parted the waves) is well under way, and the mobile barriers should be in action by 2012. For now, whenever the square floods, duckboards are laid down so that people can cross without getting wet feet. It is a novelty for tourists, but a headache for the city authorities.

Piazza San Marco, famously dubbed 'the most elegant drawing room in Europe' by Napoleon, is the focal point of Venice. It is the only square in the city important enough to be called a piazza. For most of the day, it is the domain of tourists and street-sellers, but St Mark's belongs to the citizens as well as visitors. Venetians themselves will drink at the grand cafés, even if they often save money by standing up. Before braving the hordes in the Basilica, consider splashing out on a coffee or prosecco at **Florian**, see ⑪①, prince of the city's coffee houses and ex-haunt of such literary giants as Byron, Dickens, Proust and Guardi. Linger as long as you like, preferably alfresco, to admire one of the most often-praised squares in the world.

ST MARK'S BASILICA

The centrepiece of the square is the sumptuous **Basilica San Marco** ❶ (Piazza San Marco; tel: 041-522 5205; daily 9.45am–4.45pm; charge only for Marciano Museum, Pala d'Oro and Treasury), the shrine of the Republic and symbol of Venetian glory. Before joining the queue for the Basilica (the earlier in the day you get there the better; *see box left*), take a close look at the external sculpture, mosaics and the

four horses above the central portal. These are replicas of the originals, which were looted from Constantinople during the Fourth Crusade. The spirited team of four were moved inside the Basilica to the Marciano Museum to protect them from pollution.

Myriad Mosaics

Of all the mosaics decorating the entrances and upper portals, the only original is *The Translation of the Body of the Saint* above the door on the far left. Look closely to see how the Basilica looked in the 13th century. The lower portal on the far right has a mosaic showing how the body of St Mark was taken from Alexandria, reputedly smuggled under slices of pork. Turbaned Muslims are showing their revulsion at the smell – the figure in the blue cloak is holding his nose.

The atrium mosaics are some of the finest in the Basilica: on the right **The Genesis Cupola** describes the *Creation of the World* in concentric circles, followed by scenes from the stories of Noah. Either side of the central portal are the oldest mosaics in the Basilica, *The Virgin with Apostles and Saints*.

Marciano Museum

Take the steep narrow steps up to the **Museo Marciano**, the gallery above the entrance portal. It is well worth the admission fee to see the original **bronze horses** and the views into the Basilica and over the Piazza. At first the interior appears huge, cavernous and daunting, but when your eyes have

Above from far left: the domes of the Basilica San Marco; looking down into the Piazza San Marco.

Above: gilded mosaic in the Basilica; the Campanile.

Food and Drink

① CAFFÈ FLORIAN

Piazza San Marco; tel: 041-520 5641; Thur–Tue; €€

The renowned Florian is the place for a prosecco or a Venetian spritz in style, while drowning in dubious musical offerings and watching children chasing pigeons in the square. You pay more when the band strikes up.

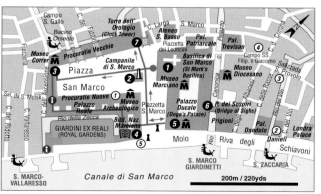

Pigeon Ban

You may notice a conspicuous absence of the famed pigeon-feed vendors in the piazza. They were banned by the city in 2008, as it was proven that the pigeon droppings were causing damage to the monuments. Anyone now seen feeding pigeons in the square faces a fine.

During the Republic, each of the bells played a different role, with one summoning senators to the Doge's Palace and another, the execution bell, literally sounding the death knell.

Below: grand exterior of the Basilica.

grown accustomed to the dim, mysterious light, it becomes exotic and entrancing. The mosaics cover some 4,000 sq m (43,000 sq ft) of floor, domes, arches and walls. The *pavimento* is like an oriental carpet, embellished with naturalistic and religious motifs, its undulations proving how movable the foundations of the church are. From the outside **Loggia dei Cavalli** you have a grandstand view of the Piazza and Piazzetta, just as doges and dignitaries did during processions and celebrations.

Back at ground level you are likely to be herded around the Basilica far too speedily to appreciate its treasures. Don't miss the first two domes in the nave for some of the finest of the mosaics: the **Pentecost Dome**, which shows the Descent of the Holy Ghost as a dove, and the **Ascension Dome,** featuring Christ surrounded by Apostles, angels and the Virgin Mary.

The Altarpiece and Other Treasures
The greatest of many treasures is the **Pala d'Oro**, a superb medieval screen behind the altar. First commissioned for Doge Pietro Orseolo in the 9th century, and increasingly enriched over the years, it is encrusted with pearls, sapphires, emeralds and enamels. Even after Napoleon's looting, there are still about 2,000 jewels left.

More Byzantine loot is stored in the **Treasury** (entered from the right transept). The prize piece here is the

Pyx, an embossed silver-gilt casket in the shape of a Byzantine church.

There are many other beautiful features in the Basilica, among them the **Baptistery** and **Zen Chapel** (both usually closed), the chapels and rood-screen. However, there is little point in trying to cover all the details in one visit.

THE CAMPANILE

The **Campanile ②** (Bell Tower; tel: 041-522 4064; daily: Apr–June and Oct–Nov 9am–7pm, July–Sept 9am–9pm, Nov–Apr 9.30am–3.45pm; often closed 3 weeks in Jan for maintenance; charge) looks much as it did when it assumed its present form in the early 16th century. This would not be surprising were it not for the fact that it collapsed in a heap on 14 July 1902. Amazingly, the only casualties were the custodian's cat and, at the foot of the tower, Sansovino's Loggetta, which was reassembled from the debris. The campanile was rebuilt exactly '*dov'era e com'era*' ('where it was and how it was'). A lift takes you to the top for stunning views of the city and lagoon, and stretching on a clear day to the peaks of the Dolomites; oddly, the canals are not visible. The plaque by the exit marks the water level on 4 November 1966 – about 0.9m (3ft) above ground level.

CORRER MUSEUM

Opposite the Basilica, on the far side of the Piazza, the **Museo Correr ③** (Piazza San Marco; tel: 041-240 5211; www.museicivicveneziani.it; daily Apr–Oct 9am–7pm, Nov–Mar 9am–5pm; charge) occupies some 70 rooms of the Procuratie Nuove (Offices of the Former Procurators of St Mark's) and the Ala Napoleonica (Napoleonic Wing). The museum is refreshingly free of crowds and full of historical and artistic treasures. Some grasp of Venetian history helps, though there are useful information sheets in English in each room. Particularly interesting are the sections devoted to the institution of the doge, Venetian trade and the Arsenale. A highlight is the Bucintoro, the ship used to transport the Doge during special processions (room 45).

Venetian Art

Art-lovers should concentrate on the **Quadreria**, a gallery of fine Venetian paintings from the 13th to the 16th centuries, including a whole room of works by the Bellinis (Room 36) and the famous Carpaccio painting *Two Venetian Noblewomen* (room 38), formerly called *The Courtesans*. The ladies look bored as they wait for their husbands to return from a hunting trip – prior to research the generous cleavages led to the mistaken identity. Also worth seeking out is the detailed wood engraving of Venice carved by Jacopo de' Barbari in 1500 (room 32).

The museum also gives you access, via rooms 18 and 19, to the **Museo Archeologico** (Archaeology Museum), full of Greek and Roman statuary. A highlight is the Grimani Altar (room 6) from the 1st century BC, with its Bacchic decoration and sensual relief of lovers in an embrace.

Above from far left: Palo d'Oro detail; the square photographed from the Campanile; the original bronze horses from above the Basilica's central portal are now in the Museo Marciano.

Museum Pass
A museum pass, covering the Palazzo Ducale, Correr Museum and all other civic museums, is available for €18 and valid for six months. A museum card for the museums of Piazza San Marco (Palazzo Ducale, Museo Correr, Biblioteca Marciana, Museo Archeologico) is available for €12 and valid for three months. To avoid the long queues, buy your tickets at the Correr Museum, which is rarely crowded. You can then enter the Palazzo Ducale without lining up again for a ticket.

Lions of Venice

The leonine symbol of Venice is everywhere. Pacific, playful or warlike, lions pose on flags unfurled over Grand Canal palaces, curl up in mosaics, fly as ensigns above ships, or crouch as statues in secret gardens. A golden winged Lion of St Mark still adorns the city standard and remains the symbol of the Veneto.

Below: the Piazzetta *(see p.35)*.

MARCIANA LIBRARY

Also accessible from the Museo Correr is the **Biblioteca Marciana** ❹ (also known as the Libreria Sansoviana; Marciana Library; tel: 041-240 7223; www. museiciviciveneziani.it; Sala Monumentali; daily Apr–Oct 9am–7pm, Nov–Mar 9am–5pm; charge), whose main hall (Sala Monumentale) has a magnificent ceiling with allegorical scenes painted by prominent artists such as Tintoretto and Veronese. The library building, which you can admire from the Piazzetta *(see p.35)* was built by Sansovino in 1530 to house the doge's precious collection of Greek and Latin manuscripts. Palladio described it as 'the richest building since antiquity'.

Sansovino was also responsible for the severe-looking **Zecca**, where Venice minted gold and silver ducats until the fall of the Republic. The mint and treasury functioned until 1870 but is now part of the Marciana Library, with the courtyard covered over and used as a reading room.

LUNCH BREAK

It is probably time for lunch and a rest from sightseeing. Everything around the Piazza is criminally overpriced. If you're happy to splurge, enjoy the stunning views from the rooftop terrace of the **Hotel Danieli**, see ⑪②; if you prefer an affordable trattoria patronised by Venetians, try **Alla Rivetta**, see ⑪③, or **All'Aciugheta**, see ⑪④, both behind the Riva degli Schiavoni.

PALAZZO DUCALE

From the 9th century to the fall of the Republic in 1797, the **Palazzo Ducale** ❺ (Doge's Palace; Piazza San Marco; tel: 041-71 5911; www.museicivicive neziani.it; daily: Apr–Oct 9am–7pm, Nov–Mar 9am–5pm; charge) was the powerhouse of Venice. It was the residence of the doges, seat of the government and venue of the law courts and prisons. By the 14th century the Venetian head of state was little more than a figurehead, or 'a glorified slave of the Republic', as Petrarch put it. But as far as living quarters went, the doge couldn't com-

plain. No other residence could rival it, and for many years this was the only building in Venice entitled to the name *palazzo*. Other grand residences had to be satisfied with the appellation Ca', short for *casa* (house).

The ceremonial entrance, on the Piazzetta, was the **Porta della Carta**, a magnificent piece of flamboyant Gothic architecture, showing Doge Foscari kneeling before the Lion of St Mark. Today this is the public exit, the entrance being the **Porta del Frumento** on the waterfront. From this side you can admire the shimmering pink façade, the delicate arches and the florid Gothic detail.

Palace Interior

Located near the entrance, the **Museo dell'Opera** (Works Museum) houses some of the original richly carved capitals from the palace. From here you go into the main courtyard, whose **Scala dei Giganti** (Giants' Staircase) formerly made an appropriately grandiose entry to the palace.

Inside the palace the great chambers were the meeting place for the highest levels of political and administrative systems. Huge rooms are decorated with heavily encrusted ceilings and monumental canvases, all in glorification of the great Venetian Republic. Leading artists of the day, including Tintoretto and Veronese, were commissioned to convey the idea that Venice was not just a place of power, but also one of overwhelming beauty.

The sumptuous **Scala d'Oro** (Golden Staircase) leads up to the doge's private apartments, then up again to the grand Council Chambers. The most impressive amongst these are the **Anticollegio**, the waiting room for ambassadors, with Veronese's *Rape of Europe* (opposite the window wall) and works by Tintoretto; the **Sala del Collegio**, with magnificent ceiling paintings by Veronese; and the **Sala del Senato**, with another elaborate ceiling, painted by Tintoretto and assistants. It was in the **Sala del Consiglio dei Dieci** that the notoriously powerful Council of 10 (in fact about 30) tried crimes against the state. Secret denunciations were posted in the *bocca di leone* (lion's mouth) in the waiting room.

Above from far left: gilded ceiling in the Palazzo Ducale; the building's exterior.

Food and Drink

② LA TERRAZZA
Hotel Danieli, Castello 4196, Riva degli Schiavoni; tel: 041-522 6480; €€€
The view alone is worth it: the rooftop terrace of this historic hotel overlooks St Mark's Basin. Highlights of the Mediterranean-inspired cuisine are the antipasti, chosen from the buffet, the fish soup and the seafood. You need to book.

③ ALLA RIVETTA
Castello 4625, Ponte San Provolo; tel: 041-528 7302; Tue–Sun; €€
Set by the bridge across the Rio del Vin, linking Campo Santi Filippo e Giacomo and Campo San Provolo, this is an unpretentious, un-touristy place close to San Marco. Fish and seafood predominate (grills and cuttlefish), as do polenta and plates of roast vegetables. Trade is brisk, the atmosphere breezy and service a touch brusque.

④ ALL'ACIUGHETA
Castello 4357, Campo Santi Filippo e Giacomo; tel: 041-522 4292; daily; €€
This unpretentious, value-for-money *bacaro* goes against type by having space, a terrace and a proper menu with plenty of choice. They also have a nice selection of decent pizzas. It's popular with Venetians, tempted by the fine Friuli wines, Adriatic fish, oysters and cheeses.

After the armoury, you go back to the second floor, along Liagò Gallery, to the grandest room of all: the **Sala del Maggior Consiglio**. This was the Assembly Hall, where doges were elected and where the last doge abdicated. The proportions are monumental – some 3,000 guests were accommodated when Henry III of France was entertained here at a state banquet in 1574. The ceiling consists of panels painted by famous contemporary artists, among them Tintoretto and Veronese, whose dynamic *Apotheosis of Venice* stands out for its dramatic perspective. Tintoretto's

huge *Paradise*, which covers the entire east wall, was for a long time the largest painting in the world: a staggering feat for a man of 70. Below the ceiling a frieze features the first 76 doges. Note the blacked-out space that should depict Marin Falier, the doge executed for treason in 1355.

Bridge of Sighs

From the splendour of the council rooms you are plunged, as were the prisoners, into the dungeons. The *pozzi*, the dungeons beneath the palace, were dark, dank and infested with rats; the *piombi*, where Casanova entertained and masterminded his daring escape, were salubrious in comparison. The new prisons, which are those you see today, are reached via the **Ponte dei Sospiri** ❻ (Bridge of Sighs) – where you can peep through the grills – named after the sighs of prisoners as they took a last look at freedom before torture or execution. Or so the story goes. In fact, by the time the bridge was built in the 17th century, the cells were quite civilised by European standards, and used only to house petty offenders. Only one political prisoner ever crossed the bridge.

The Secret Itinerary

The 'Secret Itinerary' is a fascinating guided tour, in English as well as Italian, which takes in the hidden parts of the palace, such as the torture chamber and *piombi* dungeons. Booking is essential either online at www.museicivici veneziani.it, by telephone, tel: 041-520 9070, or at the information desk of the Palazzo Ducale.

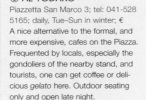

Food and Drink
⑤ AL TODARO
Piazzetta San Marco 3; tel: 041-528 5165; daily, Tue–Sun in winter; €
A nice alternative to the formal, and more expensive, cafes on the Piazza. Frequented by locals, especially the gondoliers of the nearby stand, and tourists, one can get coffee or delicious *gelato* here. Outdoor seating only and open late night.

THE PIAZZETTA

Bounded by the mint, the Basilica and the Doge's Palace is the Piazzetta (Little Square) overlooking the Molo, or waterfront. The quayside here, known as Bacino San Marco, is where foreign dignitaries and ambassadors would moor their boats as they entered the city – now you will see a lively gondola stand.

Pop into **Al Todaro**, see ⑪⑤, for a quick coffee among the gondoliers, and observe the enormous granite columns of **San Marco and San Teodoro**, brought back from Constantinople in the 12th century. One column is topped by a statue of Saint Theodore, who was the original patron saint of the city before St Mark's remains were brought to Venice from Alexandria. The other column is surmounted by what appears to be a winged lion, the traditional symbol for St Mark *(see p.32)*. It is now believed this lion is actually a chimera that was brought back from China; the Venetians simply added wings and transformed it into the lion of St Mark.

TORRE DELL' OROLOGIO

To the west of Piazza San Marco is the **Bacino Orseolo**, the main gondola depot, too busy a spot for a romantic ride but ideal for watching water traffic. The basin backs onto the **Procuratie Vecchie**, the earliest of the Procurators' offices.

At the far end of the building, over the archway, stands the **Torre dell'**

Orologio ❼ (Clock Tower; Piazza San Marco; tel: 041-520 9070; www.museicivicivenezieni. it; guided tours in English Mon–Wed at 10am, 11am and 1pm, Thur–Sun at 2pm, 3pm and 5pm; reserve ahead; charge). The Renaissance tower (1496) has a large gilt-and-blue-enamel clockface, which displays the signs of the zodiac and phases of the moon. It also, of course, tells the time, with two bronze figures of Moors striking the bell on the hour. Behind the Clock Tower, shoppers can plunge into the dark alleys of the **Mercerie**.

Gondola Rides
The Bacino Orseolo is the most central place to begin a gondola ride, but don't pay more than the official rate and agree your route and price before setting off. For romance, stick to the back canals rather than the Grand Canal. You pay extra for music or evening trips.

Below: the Piazzetta.

VAPORETTO DOWN THE GRAND CANAL

The Grand Canal sweeps majestically through the heart of the city, lined by a rich and varied parade of palaces and teeming with boats of all descriptions. You can see it all from a vaporetto (waterbus) on this tour.

Above: Ca d'Oro; vaporetto no. 1.

DISTANCE 4km (2½ miles)

TIME 40 mins on vaporetto no. 1 (30 mins if you catch no. 2)

START Piazzale Roma vaporetto

END San Zaccaria-Danieli vaporetto

POINTS TO NOTE

This ride is especially beautiful around sunset, when the light hits the buildings and most of the day trippers will have gone home, leaving you with a much less crowded ride. The faster no. 2 covers the same journey, but only makes seven stops en route. Alternatively, you could splash out on a gondola.

Waterbus Pass
Since Grand Canal tickets are €6 and only valid for 60 minutes, you might consider a pass for unlimited travel. These are available for 12 hours (€14), 24 hours (€16), 36 hours (€21), 48 hours (€26) or 72 hours (€31).

The Grand Canal, Venice's fabulous highway, is nearly 4km (2½ miles) long. The surprisingly shallow waterway is spanned by four bridges and lined by 10 churches and over 200 palaces. It sweeps through six city districts *(sestieri)*, providing changing vistas of palaces and warehouses, markets and merchant clubs, courts, prisons and even the city casino. You can see it all from vaporetto no. 1, the waterbus that takes it slowly, stopping at every landing stage.

The route starts from **Piazzale Roma ❶**, in the north of Venice. You could, of course, do it the other way round, starting from San Marco, but this way you have the grand finale of the Santa Maria della Salute church and the San Marco waterfront. Ideally do both, giving yourself more time to absorb the visual feast. You could start at the railway station (Ferrovia), but you are guaranteed the best views from a seat at the open-air front of the boat; for this, you need to be one of the first to embark, at Piazzale Roma.

PIAZZALE ROMA AND THE FERROVIA

As you ride towards the station, you'll have a good view of the **Ponte Calatrava** – Venice's newest bridge, unveiled in 2008. It was designed by acclaimed Spanish architect Santiago Calatrava and connects Piazzale Roma with the railway station. A minimalist structure of steel, glass and stone, the bridge has inevitably courted controversy, especially for its lack of wheelchair access. A lift is to be installed to resolve this issue.

Venice's **Ferroviaría Santa Lucia ❷** comes into view on your left. This striking modern building was built in

1954, with its stairway offering visitors their first taste of the Venetian lagoon. Beside the station, the Baroque church of the **Scalzi** was named after the 'barefooted' *(scalzi)* Carmelite friars who founded it in the 17th century. In 1915 an Austrian bomb hit the roof, which was decorated with a fresco by Tiepolo. Fragments of the work are now in the Accademia. The vaporetto passes under the **Ponte degli Scalzi**, built in 1934 to replace a 19th-century iron structure.

FONDACO DEI TURCHI TO THE PESCHERIA

Opposite the San Marcuola stop the **Fondaco dei Turchi ❸** was a stunning Veneto-Byzantine construction before it was heavily restored in the 19th century. The former warehouse was leased to Turkish merchants; today it is home to the Museum of Natural History. Just past the landing stage on the left, the vast **Palazzo Vendramin-Calergi ❹** is one of the canal's finest Renaissance palaces, designed by Mauro Coducci.

Wagner died here in 1883. Today, it is home to the city's casino.

Beyond the Baroque church of San Stae on your right looms the vast **Ca' Pesaro ❺**, designed by the only great Venetian Baroque architect, Baldassare Longhena. It houses a **Gallery of Modern Art** and an **Oriental Museum**. Beyond it the white Ca' Corner della Regina was the birthplace of Caterina Cornaro, queen of Cyprus, in 1454.

The vaporetto recrosses the canal to the **Ca' d'Oro ❻** landing stage, by the palace of the same name. Architecturally, this is a landmark building and a sumptuous version of a Venetian palace. The pink-and-white filigree façade, with its carved capitals, crowning pinnacles and bas-reliefs, was once covered in gold leaf – hence the name, House of Gold. The original owner, Marino Contarini, demolished a pre-existing palace to construct this magnificent building in the early 15th century, as a demonstration of his wealth and status within Venetian society. The Gothic palace houses the

Chance Your Luck
To admire the Palazzo Vendramin-Calergi from afar, leave the boat at San Stae. To gamble in the impressive casino, get off at San Marcuola. It is open all year round 3pm–2am. Dress smartly and bring your passport. Wagner's mezzanine apartments here can also be visited.

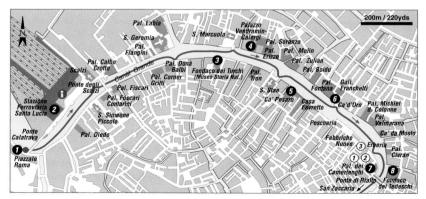

Galleria Franchetti, one of the city's most appealing art galleries *(see p.77)*.

Erberia

Look across the canal to the **Erberia**, where vegetables, fruit and flowers have been sold for centuries. The city opened a new vaporetto stop (Rialto Mercato) here in 2007 to allow locals better access to this busy central market. Barges from the island of Sant' Erasmo arrive early in the morning to offload their crates of colourful produce on the quayside.

Pescheria

Next door, fresh fish is laid out on piles of ice under the colonnades of the mock-Gothic **Pescheria** (fish market). If you have a pass and are able to hop on and off the vaporetto at your leisure, the Erberia holds many options for dining on the canal, see ⑪①, ⑪② and ⑪③.

AROUND THE RIALTO

Gondolas and traffic congestion are likely to slow you down at the **Rialto**, giving you time to take in the bridge and surrounding buildings. Just before the bridge on the right the **Palazzo dei Camerlenghi** ❼ (1528) was formerly the office of the city treasurers *(camerlenghi)*. Later, it served as the state prison. Opposite, the **Fondaco dei Tedeschi** ❽, named after the German merchants who leased the emporium, was the most important trading centre in the Rialto area. A healthy trade in precious metals from German mines meant that this privileged community created a cross between emporium, commercial hotel and social club. It is now a post office. Originally the façade was adorned with frescoes by Giorgione and Titian; the remaining fragments are now protected in the Galleria Franchetti in the Ca' d'Oro *(see p.77)*.

RIALTO BRIDGE TO CA' FOSCARI

Next you pass the **Ponte di Rialto** (Rialto Bridge; *see p.73*), constructed in 1588–91 after two of the previous wooden bridges had collapsed. Michelangelo, Palladio and Sansovino were among the eminent contenders for the

---

Food and Drink 🍴

① IL MURO
San Polo 222, Campo Bella Vienna (labelled Campo Battisti on maps); tel: 041-523 7495; Mon–Sat; €€
Il Muro makes a great stop for a cocktail or light meal. The outdoor tables are perched right by the Rialto market, where you can watch vendors unloading their wares. Try the *antipasto misto* for a sampler of delicious local seafood from the market.

② NARANZARIA
San Polo 130, Erberia; tel: 041-724 1035; Tue–Sun; €€
This stylish and modern *osteria-enoteca* is located in what was a warehouse for citrus fruit. Grab an outdoor table on the Erberia for views of the Grand Canal. Besides fresh seafood carpaccio and hot dishes, such as monkfish with saffron, the chef Akira serves up a rare treat in Venice – sushi.

③ AL BANCOGIRO
San Polo 122, Campo San Giacometto; tel: 041-523 2061; Tue–Sun; €€
A few doors down from Naranzaria and fit snugly into ancient porticoes by the busy Rialto crossing, this fashionable wine bar and new-wave *bacaro* stands on the site of the city's earliest bank. Eat *cichetti* with locals or select from the short but ever-changing menu upstairs, with dishes based on fresh produce from the nearby markets.

commission for the new stone structure, but in the end the project went to the aptly named Antonio da Ponte.

Before the San Silvestro stop, on the left, are the arcaded palaces of **Ca' Loredan** and **Ca' Farsetti**, both now occupied by the City Council. Beyond, the large, austere-looking **Palazzo Grimani** ❾ is a Renaissance masterpiece by Michele Sanmicheli. The palace now serves as the Court of Appeal.

Just before the Sant'Angelo stop, note the Renaissance **Palazzo Corner-Spinelli** ❿ (1490–1510), designed by Mauro Coducci and distinguished by its arched windows and rusticated ground floor. This became a prototype for many other *palazzi* in Venice.

Stopping at San Tomà gives you time to look across to the **Palazzo Mocenigo** ⓫. Byron lived here for two years, renting the *palazzo* for £200 a year. His affair with his housekeeper ('of considerable beauty and energy… but wild as a witch and fierce as a demon') ended with the brandishing of knives and his lover hurling herself into the Grand Canal. Right on La Volta (the bend of the canal) and recognisable by its distinctive pinnacles, **Palazzo Balbi** ⓬ was the chosen site for Napoleon to watch the regatta of 1807, held in his honour.

Ca' Foscari

On the same side, across the tributary (Rio Foscari) the **Ca' Foscari** ⓭ was described by the art critic John Ruskin as 'the noblest example in Venice of 15th-century Gothic'. It was built in 1437 for Doge Francesco Foscari; today it is a university building.

CA' REZZONICO TO THE ACCADEMIA

The next stop is **Ca' Rezzonico** ⓮, named after what is arguably the finest Baroque palace in Venice. Designed in 1667 by Baldassare Longhena, it was at one time owned by Robert Browning's reprobate son, Pen. It was while Robert Browning was staying here that he died of bronchitis. Now the **Museo del Settecento Veneziano** (Museum of 18th-century Venice; Wed–Mon 10am–6pm), it has a suitably grandiose Rococo interior, decorated with massive chandeliers, frescoed ceilings and lacquered furniture. The second floor is a picture gallery of 18th-century Venetian paintings, while the third is home to the **Egidio Martini Picture Gallery**, an eclectic collection of Venetian works spanning five centuries. In terms of Venetian art, Ca' Rezzonico takes up

Above: Ca' Foscari; gondola on the Grand Canal.

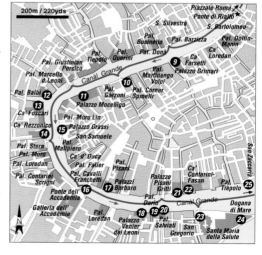

from where the Accademia *(see below and p.42)* leaves off.

Palazzo Grassi and the Accademia

Opposite the Ca' Rezzonico is the **Palazzo Grassi** ⑮. This fine example of an 18th-century patrician residence was bought in 2006 by the French business magnate François Pinault to house his huge collection of modern art *(see below)*. The palace was previously owned by Fiat, which hosted major art exhibitions here.

The wooden **Ponte dell'Accademia** ⑯ (Accademia Bridge) was built as a temporary structure in the 1930s to replace a heavy iron bridge. However, the Venetians were so pleased with it that the bridge was retained. Beside the bridge on the right is the **Accademia Gallery** *(see p.42)* – the world's greatest collection of Venetian paintings, housed in a former monastery.

PALAZZO BARBARO TO SAN ZACCARIA

Beyond the bridge, the second and third adjoining buildings on the left are the Gothic **Palazzi Barbaro** ⑰. The second was a haunt of writers and artists, when the palace belonged to the Curtis family of Boston. Among the guests here were Robert Browning, John Singer Sargent, Monet and Whistler, who both painted here, and Henry James who wrote *The Aspern Papers* here and used it as a setting for *The Wings of a Dove*. The film of the book was also shot in the palace.

Peggy Guggenheim Collection

On the right, the **Palazzo Venier dei Leoni** ⑱ or Palazzo Nonfinito ('unfinished palace') is a modern-looking building, which now houses the **Peggy Guggenheim Collection** *(see p.59)*.

François Pinault

As you float down the Grand Canal, close to the Accademia, you may notice a strange sight. In front of a classic 18th-century *palazzo* you will see a piece of contemporary art, such as a large metallic dog by Jeff Koons or a skull made of kitchen utensils by Indian artist Subodh Gupta. This is the work of François Pinault, the French billionaire and owner of Christie's auction house, who snapped up the Palazzo Grassi (San Marco 3231 Campo San Samuele; www.palazzograssi.it; tel: 041-523 1680; daily 9am–7pm) and unveiled it in 2006 as a new hub of contemporary art. Pinault's private collection of art holds 2,500 works, a small portion of which is shown on a rotating schedule here, along with other exhibitions. Pinault's takeover does not end there; he recently beat out a competing bid from the Peggy Guggenheim to overhaul the Dogana di Mare (under renovation; scheduled to open June 2009), converting it into another exhibition centre, which will allow him to display up to 20 percent of his collection and catapult Venice even further into the centre of the contemporary art world.

Palazzo Dario

Two blocks on, the palace with the coloured marble and distinctive chimneys is the charming but reputedly cursed **Palazzo Dario** ⓳, built for a Venetian diplomat. Over the centuries there has been a history of murder, bankruptcy and suicide here. The last victim was industrialist Raul Gardini, owner of the palace from 1985, who shot himself during the corruption investigations of 1993.

Palazzo Salviati

Directly after Palazzo Dario, you'll note **Palazzo Salviati** ⓴, one of the newer *palazzi* on the Grand Canal. Built in 1924, this palace was the home of a well-established glass-blowing family. They took advantage of their prime real estate to do a little advertising for themselves on the façade: note the prominent mosaic that is completely out of place with the Renaissance-style architecture.

Palazzo Pisani-Gritti

Beyond the Santa Maria del Giglio landing stage on the left, the **Palazzo Pisani-Gritti** ㉑ belonged to Doge Andrea Gritti in the 16th century. The palace became a hotel between the wars and has a roll-call of illustrious visitors. Soon after the Gritti, the tiny but exquisite **Ca' Contarini-Fasan** ㉒ is known as the House of Desdemona.

Grand Finale

Standing guard at the canal entrance is the all-pervading **Santa Maria della Salute** ㉓ *(see p.58)*, Longhena's

Baroque masterpiece with a huge, exuberant façade, scrolls and statues and a massive dome. On the tip of the promontory, the figure of Fortuna on a golden globe can be spotted on top of the **Dogana di Mare** ㉔ (customs house; currently under construction; *see p.58*).

Stay on the boat until the landing stage at **San Zaccaria** ㉕ – that way you can enjoy the stunning view of the San Marco waterfront, as well as the island of San Giorgio, before disembarking.

Above from far left: the canalside and Palazzo Barbaro, near the Ponte dell'Accademia; the Palazzo da Mosto, one of the oldest houses on the Grand Canal.

Below: looking towards Santa Maria della Salute.

THE ACCADEMIA

This treasury of Venetian art ranges from Renaissance masterpieces and Byzantine panels to vibrant ceremonial paintings, but it is as memorable for its revealing snapshots of everyday life as for its sumptuous showpieces.

TIME 2–3 hours
START/END Entrance to the Accademia
POINTS TO NOTE

The paintings in the Accademia are dependent on natural light, so choose a bright morning and arrive as early as you can. Otherwise, aim for late afternoon to avoid crowds. You can combine a visit to the Accademia with a walk around the smart Dorsoduro district (see p.57). You may find some of the rooms closed for restoration and certain paintings temporarily repositioned while work is ongoing.

Accademia Bridge
The distinctive wooden Ponte dell'Accademia is a popular meeting place for Venetians. It is a fine spot for watching water traffic and offers great views of the Grand Canal and church of La Salute.

100m / 110yds

Colour and Light
Vibrant colour, luminosity and a supreme decorative sense distinguish the work of Venetian masters. Of the Venetian school, art critic Bernard Berenson says, 'Their colouring not only gives direct pleasure to the eye but acts like music upon the moods.'

Food and Drink

① CAFFÉ BELLE ARTI
Dorsoduro 1051A, Campo della Carità; tel: 041-277 0461; daily; €
This friendly café has outdoor tables and is a nice stop for a salad, sandwich or coffee before a trip to the Accademia.

The collection of the **Accademia** (Campo della Carità; tel: 041-522 2247; www.gallerieaccademia.org; Mon 8.15am–2pm, Tue–Sun 8.15am–7.15pm; charge) is housed in Santa Maria della Carità, a complex of church, convent, cloisters and charitable confraternity. The church was deconsecrated in Napoleonic times and became a repository of work created during the Venetian Republic.

The collection is displayed in vaguely chronological order, dating from the 14th to the 18th centuries. The masterpieces are too numerous to absorb in one visit, and this itinerary concentrates on just some of the highlights. The gallery provides useful information sheets (with English translations) in each room, and audioguides are available in six languages.

The museum does not have a café or restaurant, so if you want a snack before your visit, try the **Caffé Belle Arti**, see ①①, just outside the entrance.

BYZANTINE STYLE

Room I shows the heavy influence of the Byzantine on the earliest Venetian painters. The principal exponent of the style in Venice was Paolo Veneziano. One of the most important of his works is the first exhibit, *Coronation of*

the Virgin, a polyptych (panel painting) with extravagant use of gold. Just before the steps up to Room II *(see below)*, look at the detailed rendering of figures in Michele Giambono's *Coronation of the Virgin* – a good example of the International Gothic style.

VENETIAN RENAISSANCE

Room II contains one of the most important altarpieces of the early Venetian Renaissance: Giovanni Bellini's *Madonna Enthroned with Saints* (right wall). Renaissance painting came late to Venice, brought largely through the great genius Andrea Mantegna. Giovanni Bellini was his brother-in-law and he, in turn, influenced all the Venetian painters of his own and the following generation, most of whom trained in his workshop.

Bellini Family
Bellini broke away from the traditional polyptych and brought the Virgin and saints together in a single natural composition called the *sacra conversazione* (sacred conversation). This painting had a big influence on Carpaccio's *Presentation of Jesus in the Temple* and Marco Basaiti's *Agony in the Garden*, both hanging in the same room.

Skip **Room III** and concentrate on the gems in **Room IV** and **Room V**. Giovanni Bellini was the greatest of the Venetian Madonna painters. Along with his father, Gentile, and brother, Jacopo, Giovanni commanded a large workshop that would churn out these devotional paintings. His *Madonna and*

Child with St Catherine and St Mary Magdalene (on the right as you go in) demonstrates his masterly balance of naturalness, reality and beauty. On the opposite wall, Mantegna's *St George* typifies the dry rationality of the artist's *quattrocento* style.

Follow through into **Room V** for further masterpieces by Giovanni Bellini, including the lovely *Madonna of the Little Trees* and *Madonna and Child with John the Baptist and a Saint*. In his evocative *Pietà*, he makes striking use of landscape.

Giorgione
In the same room (subject to renovation works) is one of the greatest works of the Venetian Renaissance: *The Tempest* by Giorgione. Little is known about the artist, who died of the plague when very young, but he is ranked

Above from far left: Giorgione's *The Tempest*; detail of the gallery exterior.

Reflections of Glory The Republic set great store by the State painter, with artists of the calibre of Bellini, Titian and Tintoretto expected to capture Venetian glory with vibrant depictions of ceremonial events, such as the receiving of prelates, ambassadors and dignitaries.

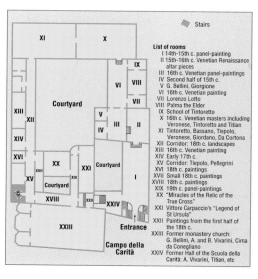

List of rooms
I 14th-15th c. panel-painting
II 15th-16th c. Venetian Renaissance altar pieces
III 16th c. Venetian panel-paintings
IV Second half of 15th c.
V G. Bellini, Giorgione
VI 16th c. Venetian painting
VII Lorenzo Lotto
VIII Palma the Elder
IX School of Tintoretto
X 16th c. Venetian masters including Veronese, Tintoretto and Titian
XI Tintoretto, Bassano, Tiepolo, Veronese, Giordano, Da Cortona
XII Corridor: 18th c. landscapes
XIII 16th c. Venetian painting
XIV Early 17th c.
XV Corridor: Tiepolo, Pellegrini
XVI 18th c. paintings
XVII Small 18th c. paintings
XVIII 18th c. paintings
XIX 19th c. panel-paintings
XX "Miracles of the Relic of the True Cross"
XXI Vittore Carpaccio's "Legend of St Ursula"
XXII Paintings from the first half of the 18th c.
XXIII Former monastery church: G. Bellini, A. and B. Vivarini, Cima da Conegliano
XXIV Former Hall of the Scuola della Carità: A. Vivarini, Titian, etc

Venice was beloved by Grand Tourists, notably the English, French and Germans. As the forerunners of souvenir-hunters, these acquisitive nobles became collectors of Venetian keepsakes, of which the most prized were paintings. Canaletto was the most popular export.

as one of the founders of modern painting. Giorgione, who trained under Bellini, was an innovator in that he achieved his effect through the use of colour and light as opposed to line and drawing. *The Tempest* is one of the artist's few certain attributions, but the subject still remains a mystery. Beside it, *The Old Woman*, by the same artist, is a striking piece of early realism.

Titian, Veronese and Tintoretto

Rooms VI–VII pave the way for the great High Renaissance works of art, introducing Titian, Tintoretto and Veronese. Titian boldly presents *St John the Baptist* as a muscular athlete in a theatrical pose. After the death of Giorgione (1510), Titian (*c.*1487–1576) went on to dominate Venetian painting throughout his long life. Brilliant use of colour and lyrical composition are the ingredients of his genius.

Typical of the first half of the 16th century are the richly coloured, exuberant paintings such as the *Sacra*

Below: Tiepolo's *Rape of Europa.*

Conversazione by Palma Il Vecchio in **Room VIII**, just beyond the bookshop. On an entirely different note is the melancholy and penetrating *Portrait of a Young Man* by Lorenzo Lotto in the adjoining room. Acute observation of personality is a notable feature of Venetian Renaissance portraiture.

Take the steps up to **Room X** for the great masterpieces of the High Renaissance. Paolo Caliari (1528–88), better known as Veronese, as he was from Verona, painted in a style of exuberant colour and realism. To your right and covering the entire wall is Veronese's grandiose *Feast in the House of Levi*. It was painted as *The Last Supper* but its hedonistic content (dogs, drunkards, dwarfs, etc) brought Veronese before the Inquisition. Rather than eliminate the offending details, however, the painter merely changed the title of the work.

Tintoretto (1518–94) was born in Venice and never moved from her shores. A man of fanatical religious conviction, he brought a kind of frenetic Mannerism to the Renaissance. His reputation was made with the striking *St Mark Rescuing the Slave.* Inspired use of shadow, foreshortening, depth and movement are typified in the dramatic *Stealing of the Body of St Mark* and *St Mark Saving a Saracen from Shipwreck*. In the same room, Titian's dark and poignant *Pietà*, bathed in mystic light, was the artist's last work, painted when he was over 90, possibly for his own tomb in the Frari. Veronese's *Marriage of St Catherine* and *Madonna Enthroned with Saints*

are radiant, richly coloured works demonstrating his use of dazzling hues.

Tiepolo

At the far end of **Room XI** you can't miss Tiepolo's grandiose tondo, *Discovery of the True Cross*, showing his mastery of illusionistic perspective.

Room XII is a gallery of light-hearted, lyrical, almost sugary landscape paintings. In the 18th century the key note in art was to delight and please the senses. Good examples are the graceful, airy *Rape of Europa* and *Apollo and Marsyas* by Tiepolo (Room XVI). As a young man Tiepolo was influenced by Giambattista Piazzetta, whose dashing use of chiaroscuro in free-handling style is seen in his masterpiece *The Soothsayer*, in the last gallery on the right.

VIEWS OF VENICE

Topographical painting, as illustrated in **Room XVII** (left, off the last gallery) was a fashion of the time. Antonio Canal, better known as Canaletto, transformed the fashion into an industry. *Perspective* is a good example of his precisely drawn scenes. Contrast Guardi's spontaneous, vibrant views of Venice. For an intimate insight into Venetian daily life in the 18th century take a look at Pietro Longhi's witty genre paintings towards the end of the room.

CEREMONIAL ART

Now you go back in time. Two left turns should bring you to **Room XX**, containing eight large canvases by five 'ceremonial artists' of the late 15th and early 16th centuries, commissioned by the Scuole Grande di San Giovanni Evangelista. The scenes, depicting the *Stories of The True Cross*, are full of historical detail, documenting Venetian life in the 15th century. Worth singling out are Gentile Bellini's *Corpus Domini Procession*, showing Piazza San Marco at the end of the 15th century and (opposite) *The Curing of a Man Possessed by Demons* by Carpaccio, showing the old wooden Rialto Bridge, which collapsed in 1524. **Room XXI** is devoted to Carpaccio's wonderfully graphic *Scenes from the Life of St Ursula*.

In the last room (**Room XXIV**, beyond the bookstall) the great triptych of Antonio Vivarini and Giovanni d'Alemagna demonstrates a combination of the International Gothic and the emerging Renaissance styles. Facing you, Titian's *Presentation of the Virgin*, still occupying its original position on the entrance wall of the gallery, makes a fitting finale to your visit.

Once you've had your fill of art, satisfy your hunger by taking a quick jaunt to **Ristorante San Trovaso**, see ⑪②, which can be reached by following Rio Terà Carità south and turning right onto Calle Larga Nani.

Above: detail of Veronese's *Feast in the House of Levi* (1573); the painting invoked the Inquisition's wrath, with its sacrilegious portrayal of buffoons, drunkards and dwarfs. Veronese sidestepped the issue by renaming his work in a more secular vein.

Religious Art
Many of the works in the Accademia come from churches that were demolished or suppressed during Napoleon's occupation of Venice.

Food and Drink

② RISTORANTE SAN TROVASO

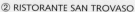

Dorsoduro 967, Calle Larga Nani; tel: 041-523 0835; Fri–Wed; €€

No-frills restaurant that serves both locals and tourists. For those looking for a post-art-viewing bite to eat, it's conveniently located near the Galleria Accademia. Try the *risotto al pescatore*, filled with delicious bits of seafood, or the hearty *pasta e fagioli* (beans).

THE *SESTIERE* OF SAN MARCO

The loop in the Grand Canal occupied by San Marco is known as 'the seven campi between the bridges', a succession of theatrical spaces, each with inviting bars and monumental palaces.

DISTANCE 3km (2 miles)
TIME 2–3 hours
START/END Piazza San Marco
POINTS TO NOTE
This walk makes a nice add on to Piazza San Marco (see walk 1). Once you get beyond Campo San Moisè, the crowds lighten considerably.

There's more to the *sestiere* of San Marco than its showpiece Piazza. The district is home to imposing churches, the legendary Fenice theatre and the parade of *palazzi* that flank the southern curve of the Grand Canal. This itinerary also explores some of the hidden quarters of San Marco, unbeknown to the hordes that cling like limpets to the central Piazza.

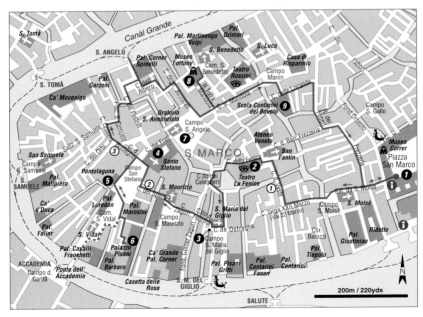

Leave **Piazza San Marco ❶** at the western end, under the arch all the way to the left. Salizzada San Moisè (where designer shopfronts such as Louis Vuitton and Gucci may well divert the eye) leads to the church of **San Moisè**. The overwhelming Baroque detail on the façade contrasts with the stark Bauer Grünwald Hotel, conspicuous as one of the city's rare modern intrusions. Cross the bridge into the Calle Larga XXII Marzo, a broad shopping street whose name refers to the day (22 March) when the patriots reclaimed the Republic from the Austrians during the 1848 uprising.

AROUND LA FENICE

Campo San Fantin

Divert right along the Calle della Veste (marked Calle del Sartor da Veste), over the bridge and into the Campo San Fantin. If you're ready for a quick and tasty meal, consider stopping in **Vino Vino**, see ⑪①, right before you enter the Campo. To your right stands the Late Renaissance church of San Fantin, to the left the rebuilt **Teatro La Fenice ❷** (Campo San Fantin; reserve guided tours at the ticket office or tel: 041-2424; charge). One of the world's loveliest opera auditoriums, it was almost completely destroyed by fire in 1838, but rose again 'like a phoenix' *(fenice)*, rebuilt almost exactly. Fire struck again in 1996. This time restorers working on the theatre were running up large debts for failing to complete the work on time, and two electricians were sentenced for arson. After eight years of

rebuilding, the theatre has been restored to its former glory. Every detail was faithfully reproduced, and the latest fire precautions installed. The reopening in 2004 was celebrated with a gala performance of Verdi's *La Traviata*.

Bordering the north of the square the **Ateneo Veneto** was once the headquarters of the Scuola di San Girolamo, a charitable body whose members chaperoned criminals to the scaffold and ensured that they were given a decent burial.

Campo Santa Maria del Giglio

Take the Calle de la Fenice on the right side of the theatre, go left under the colonnade and cross the bridge. Turn left into the little Campiello dei Calegheri, over the bridge and along the Fondamenta della Fenice, where you can see the water entrance to the opera house. The first right turning leads you into **Campo Santa Maria del Giglio ❸**, whose church of the same name (Mon–Sat 10am–5pm; Chorus Church; charge), with all its Baroque ornamentation and secular statuary, appalled the art historian John Ruskin. The church is full of paintings, including Rubens's *Madonna with Child and St John* (in the chapel on the right).

Food and Drink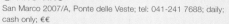

① VINO VINO

San Marco 2007/A, Ponte delle Veste; tel: 041-241 7688; daily; cash only; €€

Charming annexe to the Antico Martini restaurant that offers an excellent selection of wines by the glass, as well as a small menu. The *risotto di pesce* (fish) makes for a hearty and quick meal, though its quick exit from the kitchen means it's not made to order.

Above from left:
Sunday morning on Campo Santo Stefano; trendy *bacaro* in the San Marco area.

Christmas Fair
For the past decade Campo Santo Stefano has been home to a traditional Christmas fair that attracts the local community. If you are in town during the month of December, stop by for musical performances and booths selling regional culinary specialities and crafts.

CAMPO SANTO STEFANO

Turn right out of the square, cross over two bridges and through Campo San Maurizio, following the yellow sign for the Accademia. You will come to the large, attractively rambling **Campo Santo Stefano**. Enjoy the bustle from one of the open-air cafés, such as **Le Café**, see ②. Bull-baiting took place in the square until the early 19th century, when several spectators were killed by a falling stand. The fine Gothic church, **Santo Stefano** ❹ (Mon–Sat 10am–5pm, Sun 1–5pm; charge for sacristy), has a splendid ship's-keel roof and an inconspicuous (and normally empty) sacristy packed with dark paintings by Tintoretto and other Venetian masters.

On the western side of the **Campo Puntolaguna** ❺ is an information-packed multimedia centre (tel: 041-529 3582; www.salve.it; Mon–Fri 2.30–

5.30pm), which presents the case in favour of the MOSE dam, along with other environmental projects designed to save Venice and the lagoon.

Off the southern end of the Campo, the massive **Palazzo Pisani** ❻ houses the Conservatory of Music, where melodious strains often waft from open windows. Just beyond the Campo San Vidal make a brief detour to the **Accademia Bridge** to admire the views of the Salute church and the Grand Canal.

Return to Campo Santo Stefano and take the slim Calle delle Botteghe opposite the church, past shops, galleries and restaurants such as **Fiore**, see ③.

CAMPO SANT'ANGELO

Turn right down the Ramo di Piscina for the Piscina San Samuele. Take the steps up and cross two bridges for the Corte de l'Albero and access to the Grand Canal. The quayside here by the Sant' Angelo landing stage affords fine views of the *palazzi* opposite.

Back at Corte del' Albero, take the narrow street on the far side of the square, cross the bridge and turn right down Calle dei Avocati for **Campo Sant'Angelo** ❼, a noble quarter lined with palaces, where Casanova *(see opposite)* played his practical jokes. From here you can't fail to notice the alarming tilt of Santo Stefano's campanile.

MUSEO FORTUNY

Turn left into Calle Spezier (marked Rialto). A diversion marked to the left leads to the Late Gothic Palazzo For-

Food and Drink

② LE CAFÉ
San Marco 2797, Campo Santo Stefano; tel: 041-523 7201; daily; €
This café serves delicious cakes, as well as *panini* and *tremezzini*. It is a good spot for sipping an alfresco spritz before dinner, while enjoying the view onto the Campo. If you're visiting in the colder months, Le Café also offers a selection of teas and hot chocolate.

③ FIORE
San Marco 3461, Calle de le Botteghe; tel: 041-523 5310; Wed–Mon; €€
Not to be confused with the pricey Da Fiore *(see p.119)*, this rustic but cosy trattoria is good value considering its chic setting. It is divided into *bacaro* (traditional bar) and dining room. At the bar you will find a wide array of tasty *cichetti*. The small, 11-table restaurant specialises in Venetian cuisine that changes seasonally. If you have a sweet tooth, round your meal off with a *sgroppino* – lemon sorbet with vodka and prosecco.

tuny, former home of Mariano Fortuny. The Catalan artist, sculptor and set designer came to Venice in his 30s and spent the rest of his life in this palace. The pleated Fortuny silk dresses for which he is famed became the rage in the early 20th century. The palace now houses the **Museo Fortuny ❽** (Campo San Bento 3958; tel: 041-520 0995; www.museicivicivenezia ni.it; Wed–Mon 10am–6pm; charge) that displays Fortuny's atelier and fabrics, as well as works by contemporary artists such as Mark Rothko. The ground floor is used for temporary art installations.

CAMPO MANIN

Returning to the main Rialto route, you come to **Campo Manin**, overlooked by the starkly modern Cassa di Risparmio. Daniele Manin, who led the Venetian uprising against the Austrians in 1848, stands with his back to the bank,

looking towards the house where he lived when the rebellion was plotted.

Scala Contarini

Take the tiny street right off the Campo, signposted to the **Scala Contarini del Bovolo ❾** (Calle delle Locande 4299; closed for restoration). *Bovolo* in Venetian dialect means snail shell, and this jewel of a stairway spirals its way up the façade of the Palazzo Contarini del Bovolo. Make the detour, even during restoration; the best bit is the exterior.

BACK TO SAN MARCO

Turn right along Calle delle Locande and right again into Calle dei Fuseri. This brings you to the **Frezzeria**, a busy shopping street. Named after the arrow-makers who had their workshops here, it was notorious for its prostitutes. A left turn takes you back to the Salizzada San Moisè, near Piazza San Marco.

Above: the Museo Fortuny (top and centre); the Scala Contarini del Bovolo.

Casanova's Venice

His name may be synonymous with seduction, but Casanova (1725–98) should not be dismissed as an amorous rogue. He was an adventurer, gambler, soldier, spy, musician and man of letters, who led a dissolute life entirely in keeping with the decadence of his age. In 1755, he was arrested on charges of freemasonry and licentiousness, but managed a daring escape from the notorious Doge's Palace prisons. He then led a clandestine existence until returning to Venice in 1774, acting as a spy for the Venetian Inquisition. Casanova's Venice is still largely intact: you can see his birthplace in the romantic San Samuele quarter, or visit Campo Sant'Angelo, where he indulged in childish pranks, untying moored gondolas or summoning sleeping midwives and priests to imaginary emergencies. From his home, the city's finest clubs and salons were within easy walking distance, including gambling dens in the Frezzeria such as the Ridotto, the casino where Casanova learnt his trade.

QUIET CORNERS OF CASTELLO

Castello is a mix of sophistication and local charm. Beyond the bustle of Riva degli Schiavoni, the district offers a slice of everyday life, where dark alleys open into bright squares, flanked by some of the city's finest churches.

Above: canal near San Lorenzo; the Campanile from the Riva degli Schiavoni.

Libertine Nuns

It is hard to associate the peaceful Campo San Zaccaria with its sinister reputation for skulduggery and licence. Three doges were assassinated in the vicinity, while the adjoining Benedictine convent was a byword for lascivious living. Since noblewomen were often despatched to nunneries to save money on dowries, tales of libertine nuns were rife.

DISTANCE	1.5km (1 mile)
TIME	2–3 hours
START	Molo
END	Santi Giovanni e Paolo
POINTS TO NOTE	

This walk can easily be combined with walk 11 (done backwards) via a short walk to Santa Maria dei Miracoli.

Lying to the north and east of San Marco, this *sestiere* is the largest in Venice, and warrants two separate walks. This one explores the western side of the district and covers some of the finest art and architectural treasures in the city. Starting at the bustling waterfront close to San Marco, you work your way north through quiet streets and squares to the great Gothic church of Santi Giovanni e Paolo (San Zanipolo).

THE MOLO

Start at the **Molo ❶**, the busy waterfront to the south of the Doge's Palace, where gondolas sway by the quayside and camera-clicking crowds admire the views across the water to the shimmering island of San Giorgio

Maggiore. Pick your way through stalls of souvenirs and cross the Ponte della Paglia. Look left for the **Ponte dei Sospiri** (Bridge of Sighs; *see p.34*).

Riva degli Schiavoni

Now cross a bridge to the **Riva degli Schiavoni**, a long, curving promenade skirting the *sestiere* of Castello, and named after the Dalmatian sailors who used to moor their trading boats and barges along the waterfront. It is still a scene of intense activity, as *vaporetti*, *motoscafi*, barges, tugs and cruisers moor at the landing stages, and ferries chug across to the islands. The Riva is lined with distinguished hotels, the most historic of which is the **Hotel Danieli** *(see p.32 and 112)*. Favoured by the likes of Wagner, Dickens, Proust and Balzac, it still attracts the rich and famous.

SAN ZACCARIA

Cross over the colonnaded Ponte del Vin and take the second turning to the left, under the *sottoportego* (covered passageway) signposted to San Zaccaria. This brings you to a quiet *campo*, flanked on one side by the part-Gothic and part-Renaissance façade of the church of **San Zaccaria ❷** (Campo

San Zaccaria 4693; Mon–Sat 10am–noon, 4–6pm, Sun 4–6pm; charge). The upper section, by leading Renaissance architect Mauro Coducci, has recently been restored. In the 16th century the adjoining convent – not unlike other convents in the city – was notorious for its riotous, amoral nuns.

Inside the church, start with the chapels and crypt, reached by an entrance on the right-hand side. If closed, apply to the custodian. The Chapel of St Athanasius, with paintings by Palma Vecchio, Titian and Tintoretto, leads to the Capella di San Tarasio, the former chancel. The Vivarini family executed the glorious altarpieces, with their ornate gilded frames, which are a fine example of the Gothic painting style that was in fashion before the Renaissance took hold in Venice. The crypt, often flooded, lies below.

The greatest work of art – Giovanni Bellini's glorious *Sacra Conversazione* – is in the main church, above the first altarpiece on the left. This is one of the finest paintings in all of Venice, with Bellini creating a new type of religious painting, not based on a story from the Bible, but rather a scene where serene, meditative figures gather for a 'sacred conversation', and are integrated by soft shadow and rich, mellow hues.

SAN GIORGIO
DEGLI SCHIAVONI

Leave the church and the square via the archway. Turn right into Campo San Provolo, go under the *sottoportego* and you will come into the charming quayside of **Fondamenta dell'Osmarin**. On a corner on the far side of the canal is the red-brick Palazzo Priuli, a fine Venetian Gothic palace. At the end of the canal cross the two bridges and look right to the Greek Orthodox church of **San Giorgio dei Greci** distinguished by its dome and tall, tilting bell tower. Take the narrow alley straight ahead, pass Campiello della Fraterna on the left and join Salizzada dei Greci. The

Above from far left: gondolas moored along the Riva degli Schiavoni; Campo Santa Maria Formosa (see p.52).

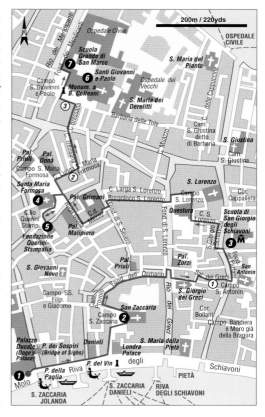

In his will, the rich and famous *condottiere* Bartolomeo Colleoni offered the city of Venice a huge sum of money if it honoured him with an equestrian monument 'in front of San Marco'. This ran contrary to Venetian tradition, but, eager to get its hands on the mercenary's fortune, the government found the answer – since the will did not stipulate the Basilica San Marco, the statue would stand in front of the Scuola Grande di San Marco instead.

Trattoria da Remigio, see ⑨①, is a good option for an authentic lunch if the mood strikes.

At the far end of the street cross over the bridge and turn left. Follow the canal along the Fondamenta dei Furlani for the **Scuola di San Giorgio degli Schiavoni ❸** (Calle dei Furiani 3259A; Apr–Oct Tue–Sat 9.30am–12.30pm, 3.30–6.30pm, Sun 9.30am–12.30pm, Nov–Mar Tue–Sat 10am–12.30pm, 3–6pm, Sun 10am–12.30pm; charge), founded by the Slavs from Dalmatia to protect their community in Venice. The tiny Scuola is decorated with an exquisite frieze of paintings by Carpaccio illustrating the lives of the Dalmatian patron saints, St George, St Tryphon and St Jerome. The scenes are rich in colour, remarkably vivid and detailed, giving a good idea of what life was like in Venice in the early 16th century.

SANTA MARIA FORMOSA

Coming out of the Scuola, cross the bridge and turn right, following the canal northwards. Shortly before a portico take a left turn down the Calle San Lorenzo for the church of **San Lorenzo**, now a hospice. Marco Polo is said to have been buried here, but his tomb was lost when the church was rebuilt in 1592. Cross the bridge at the other side of the square, turn immediately right, then first left down the Borgoloco San Lorenzo. Cross the canal of San Severo, pausing on the bridge to see some fine *palazzi*, pass under the dark and narrow *sottoportego*, carry straight on, then take a right turn

for the lovely **Campo di Santa Maria Formosa**. This charming, rambling square, once the site of bullfights and masked balls, is full of Venetian life, with market stalls and open-air cafés. It is flanked by *palazzi* and dominated by the swelling apses of Coducci's church of **Santa Maria Formosa ❹** (Mon–Sat 10am–5pm, Sun 1–5pm; charge). Art-lovers should not miss Palma il Vecchio's polyptych of *St Barbara and Saints*, adorning the chapel of the Scuola dei Bombardieri. The same artist painted portraits of Francesco and Paolo Querini, who built the 16th-century Querini-Stampalia palace south of the square. Today the building houses the **Fondazione Querini-Stampalia ❺** (Tue–Sun 10am–6pm, Fri–Sat until 10pm; charge), comprising a delightful little gallery of Venetian paintings, a library, garden and café.

If you are ready for lunch, the pizzerias in the square provide a cheerful, open-air setting. For something more authentic try **Al Mascaròn**, see ⑨②, on Calle Lunga Santa Maria Formosa, the narrow street east of the square.

Take the tiny street almost opposite Al Mascaròn, cross the quiet canal and go straight on for Campo Santi Giovanni e Paolo.

CAMPO SAN ZANIPOLO

The church of **Santi Giovanni e Paolo ❻** (daily 7.30am–12.30pm, 3.30–7.30pm; charge) is more familiarly known as San Zanipolo. This huge brick edifice vies with the Frari as the greatest Gothic church in Venice. After

the tiny streets of Castello its towering, austere form makes a dramatic impact. Known as the Pantheon of Venice, it contains the tombs of 25 doges. Identifying them is impossible without a detailed guide or the official booklet, available in the sacristy. Finest of all is Tullio Lombardo's *Monument to Doge Andrea Vendramin* (1476–8), on the left-hand side of the apse. Paintings to single out are Giovanni Bellini's *St Vincent Ferrer* polyptych, over the second altar on the right, and the Veronese ceiling paintings in the Rosary Chapel.

Scuola Grande di San Marco

The unadorned façade of Zanipolo is flanked by the ornate **Scuola Grande di San Marco** ❼, once the meeting house of silk-dealers and goldsmiths, now the civic hospital (ambulances are usually moored in the adjoining canal). Look out for the *trompe l'oeil* arches framing lions that appear to be looking from the far end of deep Renaissance porticos – in fact they are barely 15cm (6in) deep. Close by, on a pedestal, stands one of the finest Renaissance sculptures, the **equestrian statue of Bartolomeo Colleoni**, by Verrocchio *(see margin opposite)*.

At the end of your walk, enjoy some people-watching on the square at the **Antico Caffè Rosa Salva**, see ⑪③, famous for its delicious pastries and home-made *gelato*.

Above from far left: colourful window near Santa Maria Formosa; stained-glass window at the church of Santi Giovanni e Paolo.

Below left: washing day in Castello.

Food and Drink

① TRATTORIA DA REMIGIO
Castello 3416, Salizzada dei Greci; tel: 041-523 0089; Wed–Mon am; €€
This used to be a simple trattoria. It is still a local favourite, but no longer a secret. Set in a newly revitalised area, the authentic menu includes meat and grilled fish, and gnocchi is a house speciality. Service can be slow but the welcome is friendly. Book in advance.

② AL MASCARÒN
Castello 5225, Calle Lunga Santa Maria Formosa; tel: 041-522 5995; Mon–Sat; €€
An inconspicuous old-fashioned *osteria*, where you will find well-prepared snacks, excellent fish, fine wines and lots of locals. Try the fresh antipasti, the bean soup and the mixed grill; and save room for the delicious Burano biscuits dipped in dessert wine.

③ ANTICO CAFFÈ ROSA SALVA
Castello 6779, Campo Santi Giovanni e Paolo; tel: 041-522 7949; daily; €
A branch of the famous *pasticceria*, which has been around since 1879. You can snack on sandwiches or toasties for a light lunch on the square or indulge in some of their delicious pastries. Better yet, treat yourself to one of their home-made *gelato* sundaes, such as the 'Coppa Golosa' (three scoops of ice cream, fruit salad, whipped cream and strawberry syrup).

6

THE EASTERN REACHES OF CASTELLO

This leisurely stroll takes you through eastern Castello, a workaday quarter far removed from the madding crowds of San Marco, taking in a variety of lesser-known sights.

For Children
If travelling with children, the Biennale gardens present a good opportunity to see a little greenery and open space. The gardens have a small playground with swings and games, including ping-pong tables (though you must supply your own paddles and balls).

DISTANCE 2.5km (1½ miles)
TIME 2 hours
START Arsenale landing stage
END Giardini landing stage
POINTS TO NOTE

Between the Arsenale, Museo Storico Navale and Giardini Pubblici, this walk is great for families. You can arrive at the Arsenale landing via vaporetti 1 and 2.

As this area of Venice is rarely crowded, except during the Biennale, this walk is perfect for those looking to escape the masses. It begins with the Arsenale, where the great Venetian galleys were built, goes on to San Pietro di Castello, the former cathedral of Venice, and ends in the Giardini Pubblici, home to the Biennale exhibition of contemporary art.

Food and Drink

① EL REFOLO

Castello 1580, Via Garibaldi; no tel; Tue–Sun; €

This *enoteca* is the size of a large closet, but what it lacks in space, the owners make up for in charm and selection. Good choice of wines, as well as some local dishes like *bigoli in salsa* (buckwheat pasta in a sauce of anchovies and onion). A very local clientele that stands beside the bar or flows onto Via Garibaldi.

THE ARSENALE

From the **Arsenale landing stage** ❶ east of San Marco turn right (as you face inland), cross the bridge and turn immediately left. Stop on the wooden bridge over the Rio dell'Arsenale for the best views of the entrance to the **Arsenale** ❷, the old Venetian shipyard that became the symbol of Venetian maritime might *(see box on p.56)*. Heralding the shipyard is the great Renaissance gateway, guarded by stone lions plundered from Piraeus, the great shipyard in Athens, Greece. Beside the triumphal arch is a relief of Dante and a plaque recording his reference to the Arsenale in the *Divine Comedy*. The writer came here in 1306 and 1321, and the scene of frenzied activity left a lasting impression.

Naval History Museum

Back on the main waterfront stands the dignified **Museo Storico Navale** ❸ (Campo San Biagio; tel: 041-520 0276; Mon–Fri 8.45am–1.30pm, Sat 8.45am–1pm; charge). Given the tantalising elusiveness of the Arsenale, the Naval History Museum is the only place where you can fully appreciate the greatness of maritime Venice. Before its

present incarnation, the 16th-century building was used as a naval granary and biscuit warehouse. Models of Venetian craft include the original gondolas, complete with *felze* or cabin (the 'shelter of sweet sins'), and a replica of the lavish Bucintoro, the doge's state barge.

AROUND VIA GARIBALDI

Beyond the next bridge turn inland for the **Via Garibaldi ❹**. The widest street in Venice, it was created by Napoleon in 1808 by filling in the canal here. The street is lined with basic grocery shops, food stalls and friendly bars and restaurants. If you're looking to grab a glass of wine, try the small **El Refolo**, see ⑪①, where clients spill out onto the street. On the right you soon come to the unkempt end of the **Giardini Pubblici** (Public Gardens) fronted by a bronze monument to the revolutionary leader Garibaldi. Keep straight ahead for the

Rio di Sant'Anna, where you will find a colourful barge selling vegetables – one of the last surviving floating markets in the city. Take the first turning on the left (marked Calle San Gioachino). A little bridge crosses a canal festooned with laundry and flanked by brightly coloured boats. Cross a bridge into Calle Riello and then turn left for Campo di Ruga, and beyond the square on Salizada Stretta take the second turning on the right and cross the bridge for the island of San Pietro.

THE ISLAND OF SAN PIETRO DI CASTELLO

The beautiful but seriously listing campanile in front of you was the work of Mauro Coducci in 1482–8. This is the bell tower for **San Pietro di Castello ❺** (Mon–Sat 10am–5pm, Sun 1–5pm; Chorus Church; charge). It seems remarkable today that this

Above from far left: the Museo Storico Navale; Eastern Castello backstreets.

Above: Arsenale lions; the Canal d'Arsenale and the gateway into the old Venetian shipyard.

Great Explorers

On Via Garibaldi, the first house on the right, marked with a plaque, was home to the Italian explorers and navigators John Cabot and his son Sebastian, who discovered the Labrador coast of Newfoundland (mistaken at the time as the coast of China) for the English crown.

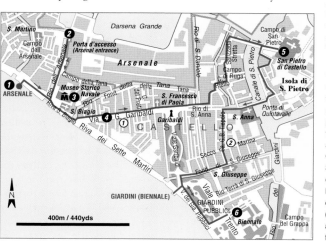

Above from left:
washing and canal houses near the Arsenale; Santa Maria della Salute, a highlight of the Dorsoduro walk.

remote church, set on a grassy square, was the Venetian seat of religious power. It was built to a Palladian design in 1557 on the site of a former castle (hence 'Castello'). Until 1807, when the bishop (later patriarch) was transferred to the Basilica of San Marco, this was Venice's cathedral.

Take the path behind the Campanile and recross the Canale di San Pietro over the Ponte di Quintavalle bridge. From here you can see boatyards and

fishing smacks. Pass the crumbling ex-church and monastery, **Sant'Anna**, on your left, then take the first left into Calle G.B. Tiepolo (which from the street is marked Campiello Correra).

Carry straight on and then turn left onto Seco Marina, where you'll find the favourite local eatery, **Dai Tosi**, see ②, a good place to stop for a spot of lunch. This is a working-class neighbourhood, and you are likely to be eating with more locals than tourists here.

From the Fondamenta San Giuseppe, turn right, heading south to the main waterfront and Giardini Pubblici. Boat enthusiasts will enjoy the waterfront here. Everything that floats, from gondolas, tugs and yachts to the large Lido ferries and ocean-going liners, seems to ply the waters of the inner lagoon.

Food and Drink

② DAI TOSI

Castello 738, Seco Marina; tel: 041-523 7102; Thur–Tue; €
A simple and pleasant trattoria and pizzeria, with tables in the garden in summer. This is conveniently located close to the Biennale, and one can even order takeaway pizzas. If you fancy something besides pizza, try the spaghetti with scampi.

In the Navy

The word *arsenale* derives from the Arabic *darsina'a*, a house of industry or workshop, a most suitable description of this Venetian production line. The Arsenale was a city within a city bounded by 3km (2 miles) of walls, with wet and dry docks and ordnance depots that were envied abroad. It was also an armaments site. At its peak this was the greatest shipyard in the world, with 16,000 *'arsenalotti'* churning out galleys on an assembly line. The fastest time was recorded in 1574, when Henry III of France visited the city. The workers created an entire galley in the time it took him to consume a state banquet. The shipyard was destroyed by Napoleon in the late 18th century, and the cannons and bronzes melted down to create monuments celebrating the French Revolution. Sadly, most of the Arsenale is closed to the public. However, if you are here during the Biennale *(see p.21)*, you can visit the colossal Corderie (rope factory) and other renovated warehouses that are used effectively to display modern art.

LA BIENNALE

If you happen to be here in an odd-numbered year between June and November, join the glamorous art crowd at the **Biennale** ❻, a highlight of the international art calendar. More than 30 permanent pavilions within the gardens display contemporary art from different nations. Although for much of the rest of the time the pavilions remain empty, they are at least now used for other temporary events such as the Biennale dell'Architettura, which is held in the intervening years between September and November.

From the Giardini landing stage you can jump onto a no. 2 vaporetto going westwards and enjoy the sublime views as you head back to San Marco.

DORSODURO

Stroll along the Zattere quayside, visit galleries in the chic eastern quarter of the Dorsoduro, then divert to one of Venice's liveliest squares. End by going off the beaten track to visit two of the region's loveliest churches.

Dorsoduro simply means 'hard back', so called because the district occupies the largest area of firm land in Venice. It is the most attractive quarter for idle wandering, with wisteria-clad walls, secret gardens and distinctive domestic architecture. Apart from the Accademia and La Salute church, the district is surprisingly free from visitors. The southern spur of the Zattere makes the most enchanting Venetian promenade.

THE ZATTERE

Start at the **Zattere landing stage ❶**, which is serviced by the no. 2, as well nos 51 or 52 from the station. The Zattere, which means floating rafts – from the days when cargo was offloaded here – is a long, spacious quayside that will lure you with its open-air cafés and canalside views. If the urge for an ice cream takes you, stop at **Nico**, see ⑪①. From here, turn right onto the Fondamenta Nani, which affords a good view, across the canal, of the **Squero di San Trovaso ❷**, one of the last surviving gondola workshops. The construction of a gondola is highly complex, involving 280 pieces of timber, cut from nine different types of wood. The boats constantly come in for scraping, tarring and overhauling – but, as at the other *squeri*, there are

only around four new gondolas constructed here each year. The craftsmen used to come from the Dolomites, hence the Alpine look of the *squero*.

The next stop on the Zattere is the church of the **Gesuati ❸** (Fondamenta Zattere ai Gesuati; Mon–Sat 10am–5pm; Chorus Church, *see p.13*; charge), just east of the landing stage. The grandiose church is a supreme example of 18th-century Venetian architecture

DISTANCE 3.5km (2¼ miles)
TIME 4–5 hours
START Zattere landing stage
END San Basilio landing stage
POINTS TO NOTE

This walk can be combined with San Giorgio and the Giudecca (walk 8) by taking the no. 2 vaporetto from the Giudecca Palanca stop to the Zattere.

Above: domestic, down-tempo Venice; pulpit detail, Angelo Raffaele, Dorsoduro.

Gondola Craftsmen
El Felze is an association of artisans who make gondolas and gondola-related items. Founded by Roberto Tramontin, owner of the Trovaso *squero*, they often organise events, and their website (www.elfelze.com) is a treasure trove of information about gondola design and production, also listing addresses for gondola workshops.

Food and Drink 🍴
① NICO
Dorsoduro 922, Zattere; tel: 041-522 5293; Fri–Wed; €
Nico is one of the best places for *gelato* and specialises in the wickedly calorific *gianduiotto* (chocolate hazelnut with whipped cream). There are a small number of tables outside if you want to eat your cool treat while enjoying the view.

Festa della Madonna

The Feast of the Salute, when a temporary wooden bridge is laid down over the Grand Canal to connect La Salute basilica with the San Marco neighbourhood, is held each year on 21 November. Venetians then traditionally cross this bridge to pay homage to the Virgin Mary and pray for good health.

which holds Tiepolo masterpieces (1739) in their original setting. Further on is **La Calcina Pensione**, otherwise known as Ruskin's House. The art historian stayed here when it was a simple inn, frequented by artists.

Follow the quayside, past the Casa degli Incurabili, a former hospice and now a children's home, the (invariably closed) Spirito Santo church and the Magazzini del Sale (Salt Warehouses), used for art exhibitions. For refreshment, stop at **Linea d'Ombra**, see ⑪②.

PUNTA DELLA DOGANA

At the tip of the peninsula, you come to the **Dogana di Mare ❹**, the 17th-century customs house, currently undergoing restoration to be converted into a modern art gallery for the display of around 140 works from the

contemporary art collection of French tycoon François Pinault *(see p.40)*. The museum is scheduled to open in June 2009. Facing St Mark's Basin, a porticoed corner tower is crowned by two bronze Atlases supporting a golden globe, with the weathervane figure of Fortuna perched on the top.

SANTA MARIA DELLA SALUTE

Rounding the peninsula, you come to Longhena's monumental church of **Santa Maria della Salute ❺** (Campo della Salute; 9am–noon, 3–6.30pm, until 5.30pm in winter; church free, charge for sacristy), erected to commemorate the deliverance of Venice from the plague of 1630. A Baroque church of massive proportions, it took over half a century to build and is sup-

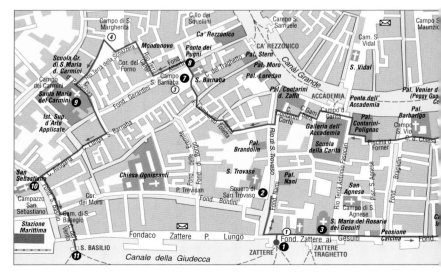

ported by over a million timber piles. After the exuberance of the façade, the grey-and-white interior is surprisingly severe. The highlights are the works by Tintoretto and Titian in the sacristy (often open only in the afternoon).

GUGGENHEIM

Back in Campo della Salute, cross the tiny bridge (marked 'Guggenheim Collection') to the Campo San Gregorio, where the deconsecrated Gothic brick church of **San Gregorio** is now used as a workshop for restoring paintings. Continue to the little Campiello Barbaro, overlooked by the ill-fated Palazzo Dario (*see p.41*) and on over a bridge to the Palazzo Venier dei Leoni, housing the **Peggy Guggenheim Collection** ❻ (enter Calle S. Cristoforo or Fondamenta Venier dei Leoni 701; tel: 041-240 5411; www. guggenheim-venice.it; Wed–Mon 10am–6pm; charge). Peggy Guggenheim (1898–1979), the eccentric American heiress, bought the palace in 1949 and lived here until her death.

The city's most visited gallery after the Accademia, it has a collection featuring works from almost every modern art movement of the 20th century. The majority of the works came directly from the artists, many of whom she patronised, befriended, entertained and – in the case of Max Ernst – married. Picasso, Pollock, Magritte, Mondrian, Brancusi and Giacometti are just a few of the big names. The collection is not huge, but it's a light, airy and welcoming sort of place, with well-displayed canvases, a sculpture garden and good café.

CAMPO SAN VIO

Following the route eastwards along the Fondamenta Venier dei Leoni you come to **Campo San Vio**, one of those rare squares in Venice where you can sit on a bench and watch the bustle on the Grand Canal. It's a short walk from here to Campo della Carità and the **Accademia** (*covered in Walk 3; see p.42*), a treasure house of Venetian art that you should save for another day.

(*see p.41*) ... (*covered in Walk 3; see p.42*)

Above from far left: the Punta della Dogana; the view across to Giudecca from Dorsoduro.

Guggenheim Garden
The sculpture-lined gardens of the Peggy Guggenheim Art Museum feature works by Henry Moore and Marino Marini; new works continue to be acquired. The garden is also where Peggy Guggenheim's ashes were laid to rest, next to where she buried her 'beloved babies', her Lhasa Apso lapdogs: Cappucino (1949–53), Pegeen (1951–3), Peacock (1952–3), Toro (1954–7), Madam Butterfly (1954–8), Foglia (1956–8), Baby (1949–59), Emily (1945–60), White Angel (1945–60), Sir Herbert (1952–65), Sable (1958–73), Gypsy (1961–75), Hong Kong (1964–78) and Cellida (1964–79).

Food and Drink

② LINEA D'OMBRA

Dorsoduro 19, Ponte dell'Umiltà, Zattere; tel: 041-520 4720; Thur-Tue; €€€

Facing the Il Redentore church on the Giudecca, this romantic restaurant and wine bar is perfect on a summer's evening, especially if you can secure a table on the floating raft. It serves reinterpreted Venetian classics, with good wines. Book in summer.

Above: gondola yard on Rio San Trovaso, Dorsoduro; San Giorgio Maggiore's cloisters from above.

Floating Market
On the far side of the Ponte dei Pugni, you can see a colourful barge crammed with fresh fruit and vegetables – one of the last of Venice's floating markets.

WESTERN DORSODURO

Passing through Camp della Carità, zigzag along the streets beyond the Accademia, and cross the Rio di San Trovaso at the first bridge. Follow the general flow to **Campo San Barnaba** ❼, passing small shops and artisans' studios. This *campo* was traditionally a quarter for impoverished nobility. You might stop for lunch at **Oniga**, see ③, on the square here.

Ponte dei Pugni

Exit out of the north end of the square, turning left onto Fondamenta Gerardini and crossing the first bridge, known as the **Ponte dei Pugni** ❽ (Bridge of Fists). The marble footprints on the bridge mark the starting spot for fist-fights between the Nicolotti, inhabitants of the parish of San Nicolò, and the Castellani, those of Castello. Originally there were no railings on the bridge, and opponents would throw each other into the canal. After several fatalities the fights were banned in 1705.

The Carmini

Carry on straight down Rio Terrà Canal, where you will pass the mask shop, **Mondonovo**, at no. 3063. A left at the end of the street leads into Campo di Santa Margherita. This rectangular 'square' is bustling with local life, and is normally full of university students from the nearby Ca' Foscari University. **Bar Rosso**, see ④, is especially good for a late-night spritz.

At the far end of the square is the church and *scuola* of the **Carmini** ❾ (Campo Carmini; church: Mon–Sat 2.30–5.30pm; free; *scuola*: daily 10am–5pm; charge). The *scuola* houses Tiepolo's sensational ceiling painting *St Simon Stock Receiving the Scapula of the Carmelite Order from the Virgin*.

San Sebastiano

Exiting the church, go right down Calle della Pazienza, cross the first bridge, and then turn right onto Calle Lunga San Barnaba, leading to the church of **San Sebastiano** ❿ (Campo San Sebastiano; Mon–Sat 10am–5pm; free), accessed across a tiny bridge. The church is a virtual museum of Paolo Veronese, its ceilings, frieze, choir, altar, organ doors and sacristy decorated with the artist's glowing and joyous works of art. This was Veronese's parish church, and, fittingly, he is buried here.

Cross the bridge out of the square and follow the Fondamenta San Basilio south to the Zattere. A no. 2 vaporetto from **San Basilio** ⓫ will take you either back to San Marco or via the Stazione Marittima towards the north of the city.

Food and Drink 🍴

③ ONIGA
Dorsoduro 2852, Campo San Barnaba; tel: 041-522 4410; Wed–Mon; €€
A friendly little restaurant with an affordable menu and seating on the square. Its seasonal menu includes both Venetian specialities and good vegetarian options.

④ BAR ROSSO
Dorsoduro 2963, Campo di Santa Margherita; tel: 041-528 7998; daily; €
One of the best-known bars on the square and great for a daytime *panini* or toasted sandwich. Late at night it is a popular hangout for the university crowd and a lively spot for a spritz.

SAN GIORGIO MAGGIORE AND THE GIUDECCA

Enjoy vistas of familiar Venetian landmarks, as the vaporetto chugs across the Canal of San Marco to the island of San Giorgio Maggiore. Then head towards the Giudecca, taking in grand views across the Giudecca canal and fine architecture by Palladio.

San Giorgio is the closest of the lagoon islands to the city, and the only major island untouched by commerce. Seen from afar, the majestic monastery appears suspended in the inner lagoon, with its cool Palladian church matched by a bell tower modelled on that of San Marco. Together with the Baroque beacon of La Salute, these two great symbols guard the inner harbour of Venice. Giudecca, just off Dorsoduro, is also celebrated for its Palladian church, while Elton John's Gothic home is a more recent addition to the list of land-

DISTANCE 3km (2 miles)

TIME 2 hours

START San Zaccaria vaporetto

END Giudecca-Palanca vaporetto

POINTS TO NOTE

This walk is especially pleasant done from late afternoon to early evening, in order to see the sunset across the Giudecca canal. Just be sure to time it, so you will still be able to see the interiors of the churches.

Jewish Community
The name Giudecca was derived either from the community of Jews who lived here or from the word '*giudicati*' or 'judged', dating from the time when troublesome nobles were banished here.

Below: view across the Grand Canal from San Giorgio Maggiore.

The Seventh
Sestiere
Traditionally, the six *pettini* ('combs' or prongs) on the prow of a gondola represent the six *sestieri* of Venice. The Giudecca is represented as the 'seventh' *sestiere* by the long strip at the top.

marks. Locals credit the rock star with turning the tide in this old working-class district, which is undergoing a rebirth with the restoration of residential and industrial buildings.

SAN GIORGIO MAGGIORE

From the **San Zaccaria** ❶ landing stage near San Marco, it is just a short jaunt on a no. 2 vaporetto (going clockwise) to San Giorgio Maggiore. The island was given to the Benedictines in the 10th century, and their monastery was one of the most important in the city. Seen from San Marco, the island sits stage-like in the inner lagoon, set off by its soaring campanile. The vaporetto will drop you directly in front of the church, with its typical Palladian façade modelled on an ancient temple.

Started by Palladio in 1566, and finished after his death in 1610, **San Giorgio Maggiore** ❷ (May–Sept 9.30am–12.30pm, 2.30–6.30pm, Oct–Apr until 4.30pm; church free, charge to climb bell tower) is cool, spacious and

perfectly proportioned. It is also home to two powerful works by Tintoretto: *The Last Supper* and *Gathering of the Manna*, both executed when the artist was almost 80. For one of the most impressive panoramas in Venice, have a monk accompany you in a lift to the top of the campanile. The view is even more spectacular than that from Piazza San Marco's across the water.

FONDAZIONE CINI

Coming out of the church, take a right out of the *campo* and follow the unmarked *fondamenta* until you reach Palladio's adjoining monastery, now the **Fondazione Cini** ❸ (tours Sat–Sun 10am; tel: 041-271 0229; www.cini.it). The building houses a foundation for the study of Venetian civilization, and also hosts contemporary art exhibits, concerts, as well as film and lecture series. On guided tours, you can visit the cross-vaulted refectory, Longhena's library and the Palladian Cloister of the Cypresses. The cloisters lead to the

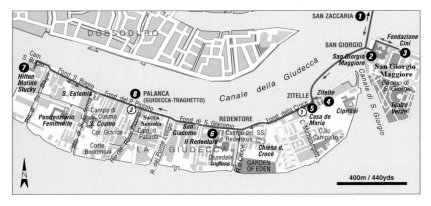

monastic gardens and the Teatro Verde open-air theatre; this pastoral setting provides an atmospheric stage set for occasional summer concerts.

THE GIUDECCA

Pick up a second no. 2 vaporetto heading westwards – they go about every 10 minutes. The boat makes three stops on the island of La Giudecca. This working-class suburb of Venice has been undergoing a gradual revamp, with the restoration of factories, houses and palaces, fashionable flats selling to foreigners and artists moving into redundant buildings.

The Zitelle

Disembark at the first stop, Zitelle, directly in front of the church of the same name. The **Zitelle** ❹ (Fondamenta delle Zitelle; Sun at 10am for mass only) was designed by Palladio, though completed after his death. The adjoining buildings, which now form the Bauer Palladio hotel, originally pro-

vided shelter for young women without a dowry and taught them lacemaking. Behind the Zitelle is the luxurious Hotel Cipriani *(see p.115)*, normally accessed by private boat.

Casa de Maria

Just right of the church you will find the most innovative building on the Giudecca, the **Casa de Maria** ❺. Built between 1910 and 1913, this elaborate building was named after its architect, a painter from Bologna called Mario de Maria. The patterned brickwork façade is reminiscent of the Palazzo Ducale, while the three luminous windows are a modern hybrid of traditional Venetian Gothic architecture. Continue west down the Fondamenta until you reach **I Figli delle Stelle**, see ⑪①, a nice stop for lunch.

Above from far left: washing in a residential street in Giudecca; lion and Il Redentore church.

Favourite Colour
'Of all the colours, none is more proper for churches than white, since the purity of the colour, as of life itself, is particularly satisfying to God.'
Palladio

Below: interior of San Giorgio Maggiore, a Palladian masterpiece.

Food and Drink 🍴
① I FIGLI DELLE STELLE
Giudecca 70/71, Fondamenta delle Zitelle; tel: 041-523 0004; Tue–Sun lunch; €€
Sleekly decorated in minimal brown and white tones, the best feature of this new restaurant is the spectacular view across the Giudecca canal. The menu features specialities from Puglia (where the chef comes from). Try the *frittura di pesce e verdure*, a delicious serving of lightly battered seafood and vegetables. Reserve for outdoor seating.

Above from left:
Molino Stucky;
Tintoretto's *The
Assumption of the
Virgin*, in the Scuola
di San Rocco, in the
San Polo district.

Il Redentore

A small bridge on the Fondamenta leads to the Campo del Sanitissimo Redentore and one of Venice's most conspicuous landmarks. Palladio's **Il Redentore** ❻ (Mon–Sun 10am–5pm), church of the Redeemer, was built to commemorate the deliverance of Venice from the 1576 plague, which took 50,000 lives. This graceful church is the scene of Venice's most beguiling festival *(see box below)*. The interior, strikingly stark and solemn, is a fine example of classical rationality.

Molino Stucky

Continue westward, passing over the Ponte Longo. Note all the boats moored along this canal and glance southward, where you might be able to make out the artificial island of **Sacca Sessola**, also known as the Island of Roses. You will soon come to the Palanca vaporetto stop, where you can stop for a drink or light meal at the rustic **Alla Palanca**, see ⑪②. This stretch of the Fondamenta is particularly lively and dotted with shops.

After another bridge, you will come to no. 805, the **Fortuny Factory** (Mon–Fri 9am–12.30pm, 2–5pm), which has been churning out Fortuny fabrics *(see p.18)* since 1922. Next door is the **Molino Stucky** ❼ building, recently converted into a 380-room hotel. The enormous neo-Gothic brick building was built in 1895 as a grain silo, pasta factory and flour mill. The mill closed in the 1950s, and lay vacant for decades until the grand opening of the **Hilton Molino Stucky** *(see p.115)* in 2007.

Back to the Main Island

From here, backtrack to the **Palanca landing** ❽ to catch the no. 2 vaporetto back to the main island. If you're lucky, you might be able to catch the Hilton shuttle ferry, which leaves passengers near Piazza San Marco.

Feast of the Redeemer

La Festa del Redentore, held on the third Sunday of July, is the most touching and intimate of Venetian festivals. It focuses on Il Redentore, the Palladian church built as a token of thanks after salvation from the plague of 1576. Then, as now, Venetians wend their way to the church carrying candles and reciting the rosary. A sweeping bridge of boats stretches across the Giudecca canal to the church, enabling people to attend Mass and listen to the chanting monks. The firework display on the eve of the feast day has been a feature since the 16th century. At night, crowds line the Zattere and the Giudecca or take to boats of every description, laden with festive picnics. From stately yachts to refuse barges and gondolas, the watercraft are bedecked in finery to create a fabulous night spectacle. Foghorns are sounded and festival fireworks blaze over the lagoon.

Food and Drink

② ALLA PALANCA
Giudecca 448, Fondamenta del
Ponte Piccolo; tel: 041-528 7719;
Mon–Sat lunch only; €€
Located not far from the Palanca
vaporetto landing, this local bar-
trattoria serves up a short lunchtime
menu. Grab one of the outdoor
tables and observe the comings
and goings over a plate of risotto
in cuttlefish ink.

SAN POLO AND SANTA CROCE

Stroll through the quiet neighbourhoods of San Polo and Santa Croce, a warren of alleys and homely squares that hide the great treasures of Bellini, Titian and Tintoretto in the Frari and Scuola di San Rocco.

San Polo and Santa Croce form adjoining districts curved into the left bank of the Grand Canal. Together they encompass the bustling Rialto market (covered in the next walk; *see p.70*) and the picturesque backwaters towards the station, centred on the quintessential *campo* of San Giacomo dell' Orio.

SCUOLA DI SAN ROCCO

This circular tour begins and ends at the **San Tomà vaporetto ❶**. Heading north from here, take the second right into the small Campo San Tomà. Over on the far side of the square you will see the former Scuola dei Calegheri, once the confraternity of the shoe-makers and cobblers. The building is now used as a public library. Follow the signs for the Scuola di San Rocco, one of the greatest city sights.

The **Scuola Grande di San Rocco ❷** (Salizzada San Rocco; tel: 041-523 4864; www.scuolagrandesanrocco.it; daily Apr–Oct 9am–5.30pm, Nov–Mar 10am–5pm; charge) is the grandest of the *scuole*, or charitable lay fraternities, and acts as a backdrop for Baroque recitals. The society is dedicated to St Roch, the French saint

of plague victims, who so impressed the Venetians that they stole his relics and canonised him.

The 16th-century building is also a shrine to the great Mannerist painter Tintoretto. He was one of several eminent contenders for the decoration of the Scuola, Veronese among them; but Tintoretto caught his competitors unawares by producing a completed painting, rather than the requested cartoon. He worked on the Scuola on and off for 24 years, producing powerful biblical scenes. As you go round, note the artist's extraordinary ability to convey theatrical effect through contrasts of light and shade, bold

DISTANCE	2.5km (1½ miles)
TIME	3–4 hours
START/END	San Tomà vaporetto
POINTS TO NOTE	

As these neighbourhoods are relatively quiet, this makes a great walk for the weekend, when others make a beeline for Piazza San Marco. It can be linked with Dorsoduro *(see walk 7)* by doing the route in reverse and heading south into Campo Santa Margherita after the Scuola di San Rocco.

The Scuole

The *scuole* were charitable lay associations, which looked after members' spiritual, moral and material welfare. Serving the citizen class from lawyers and merchants to skilled artisans, the *scuole* were expected to support the State and contribute to good causes. For the merchant class, excluded from government, this was an opportunity to show civic pride.

Titian

Titian (c.1487–1576), the great master of Venetian painting, was actually born on the mainland in the small town of Pieve da Cadore. He was sent to Venice at a young age to study painting and spent the rest of his life here until his death, aged 89. His greatest paintings are in the Frari.

foreshortening, visionary effects of colour and unusual viewpoints.

In the lower hall the paintings illustrate scenes from the *Life of the Virgin*, while the upper hall has paintings over 4.8m (16ft) high, depicting scenes from the *Life of Christ* and, on the ceiling, images from the Old Testament. Use the helpful mirrors provided to view the ceiling without straining your neck.

At the far end of the Sala dell' Albergo, scenes from *The Passion* culminate in *The Crucifixion* itself, fittingly the largest, most moving and dramatic painting of the collection. *The Glorification of St Roch* on the ceiling of the same room was the work that won Tintoretto the commission.

THE FRARI CHURCH

Retrace your steps to the Salizzada San Rocco, stopping for a pick-me-up *gelato* at **Millevoglie**, see ⑪①. From here you can see the apse end of the **Frari Church ❸** (Campo dei Frari; Mon–Sat 10am–5pm, Sun 1–6pm; Chorus Church, *see p.13*; charge), which abuts Campo San Rocco. Follow the side of the church around, taking in its simple Gothic brick façade before entering.

Along with the church of Santi Giovanni e Paolo *(see p.52)* in Castello, the Frari is the finest Gothic church in Venice. The hulking bare-brick building and adjoining monastic cloisters were built in the 14th and 15th centuries by Franciscan friars, whose first principle was poverty – hence the meagre decoration of the façade. The soaring bell tower is the tallest in Venice, after the campanile in Piazza San Marco *(see p.31)*. It is currently being restored, after instability was detected in 2006.

The Interior

Inside, the eye is drawn to Titian's gloriously rich *Assumption of the Virgin*, which crowns the main altar. On the left side of the church the same artist's *Madonna di Ca' Pesaro* is another masterpiece of light, colour and harmony, and a very daring work in that it was one of the earliest to show the Madonna out of the centre of the composition. Members of the Pesaro family, who commissioned the work, can be seen in the lower half of the painting. Directly opposite is Titian's mausoleum, erected 300 years after his death.

Other outstanding works of art here include Giovanni Bellini's beautiful *Madonna and Child with Saints* in the sacristy, of which Henry James wrote, 'Nothing in Venice is more perfect than this'; the finely carved 15th-century monks' choir; the wooden statue by Donatello of St John the Baptist on the altarpiece to the right of the main altar; and the sinister monument to Canova (to the left of the side door).

SCUOLA DI SAN GIOVANNI EVANGELISTA

Back in Campo dei Frari, cross the bridge out of the square and turn left onto Fondamenta dei Frari. Cross another bridge, turn left, and then right onto Calle del Magazen and the **Scuola di San Giovanni Evangelista** ❹. The church is part of a labyrinthine quarter of narrow alleys *(calli)* and covered passageways *(sottoporteghi)*. Though the Scuola is only open by appointment (tel: 041-718 234; www.scuolasangiovanni.it), the exterior courtyard is quite lovely. Established in 1261, the Scuola was one of the six major confraternities, largely due to its ownership of a piece of the True Cross, and played a leading role in the ceremonial life of the city.

Highlights

The first courtyard has a marble screen designed by Pietro Lombardo, which is watched over by an eagle, the evangelical symbol for St John, the confraternity's patron saint. The second courtyard features a relief of the members of the confraternity kneeling before St John. The inscription below records the purchase of the land for the Scuola in 1349.

SANTA CROCE

Exiting the courtyard, turn left and stroll down the street, soaking up the local flavour in this quiet section of town. A little way along, look out for a small courtyard on the right with a terracotta pavement laid in a herringbone pattern. At one time, most of Venice's streets were paved in this fashion. At the end of the street, turn left and cross the bridge over the canal, entering into **Campiello del Cristo**.

We are now in the *sestiere* of Santa Croce. Though centrally located, this district is bypassed by the majority of tourists, probably because of its lack of 'big name' sites. But thankfully this affords the opportunity to enjoy a slice of real Venetian life. The bridge offers a nice view of an enclosed garden with large trees, evidence that many homes do contain gardens, even in Venice.

Go straight through the *campiello*, continuing on until you arrive in Campo San Nazario Sauro. Heading east out of the square via the Ruga Bella brings you to **Campo San Gia-**

Above from far left: the Frari is the largest of all the Venetian Gothic churches; detail of TIntoretto's *Glorification of St Roch* (San Rocco), in the Scuola di San Rocco; tourists stopping on the Ponte dei Frari.

Above: Campo San Giacomo dell' Orio; marble screen, Scuola Grande di San Giovanni Evangelista.

Food and Drink
① GELATERIA MILLEVOGLIE
San Polo 3033; Salizzada San Rocco; tel: 041-524 4667; daily until late; €
Millevoglie (behind the Frari church) is reputed to be the area's best ice-cream parlour – a good enough reason to seek it out on a sweltering day. Try the fig and tiramisu flavours.

Above from left: tempting fresh pastries in the window of a *pasticceria*, in the San Polo and Santa Croce area; carnival masks.

Off the Beaten Path Linger for a drink in the friendly San Polo neighbourhood. Calle della Madonetta is a pleasant alley that runs over bridges and under buildings towards the Rialto. This is one of several adjoining streets with overhanging roofs, a rarity in Venice.

como dell'Orio **⑤**. Here you will find Venetians young and old gathering to chat in the cafes, gossip on the red benches or shop at the small grocer here. Take the time to relax, maybe join the locals for a drink at **Al Prosecco**, see ⑪②, or settle in for a meal at **Il Refolo**, see ⑪③.

PALAZZO MOCENIGO

The tour now begins to loop back to San Polo. Exit from Campo San Giacomo dell'Orio via the road that runs next to Al Prosecco. Follow the signs to the vaporetto and you will soon reach **Palazzo Mocenigo ⑥** (Salizada S. Stae 1992; tel: 041-721 798; www.museiciviciveneziani.it; Tue–Sun 10am–5pm, until 4pm in winter; charge), ancestral residence of one of the greatest dogal families and now home to a textiles museum. Fashion-lovers will adore this small collection

of Venetian period costume, mainly from the 18th and 19th centuries. It is also a great chance to view a 17th-century palatial mansion, with its opulent furnishings intact, and the family portrait gallery of a dynasty that produced seven doges.

CAMPO SAN POLO

Exiting the *palazzo*, take a left and continue along the street that led you here, cross over two bridges, then turn right into Campo Santa Maria Mater Domini. Cross the *campo*, taking the street as far as you can before turning left onto Rio Terà Bernardo. Following the street south will lead you directly into **Campo di San Polo ⑦**, the largest square in Venice after Piazza San Marco. It has none of the grandeur of San Marco but is nonetheless beautiful in its own busy way. Once the site of bull-baiting, tournaments, masked balls and fairs, it is now the scene of less festive activities such as football and cycling. You might decide to have lunch on the square at this point, at **Antica Birreria la Corte**, see ⑪④; this is also a good late-night option, if you'd prefer to come back another time.

Highlights

The **church of San Polo ⑧** (Mon–Sat 10am–5pm; Chorus Church, *see p.13*; charge) is worth a visit for the cycle of the *Stations of the Cross* by Tiepolo (follow the sign for the Crucis del Tiepolo) and Tintoretto's *Last Supper*.

Next to the church, the classical **Palazzo Corner-Mocenigo** was for a

---

Food and Drink

② AL PROSECCO

Santa Croce 1503, Campo San Giacomo dell'Orio; tel: 041-520 222; Mon–Sat; €€

Friendly owners Stefano and Davide run this small *enoteca* on the square. A rotating selection of wines by the glass are available, as well as a good selection of cheeses, *salumi* (cold cuts) and salads.

③ IL REFOLO

Campiello del Piovan, Campo San Giacomo dell'Orio; tel: 041-524 0016; closed all day Mon and Tues lunch; €–€€

In a pretty canalside setting, this innovative, upmarket pizzeria is the place for a peaceful meal. Classic as well as creative pizzas.

④ ANTICA BIRRERIA LA CORTE

San Polo 2168, Campo San Polo; tel: 041-275 0570; daily; €€

Good value with outdoor seating and ample indoor seating, making this a great stop for large groups. It offers a nice range of inventive salads and pizzas and opens relatively late for the area.

while the residence of Frederick Rolfe (self-styled Baron Corvo), the notoriously eccentric English writer. It was here that he wrote *The Desire* and *Pursuit of the Whole*, ruthlessly lampooning English society in Venice. As a result his host threw him out, penniless, onto the streets. On the opposite side of the square is the **Palazzo Soranzo** with its sweeping pink Gothic façade.

MASK SHOPS

Turn right out of the church and cross the bridge. Along **Calle dei Saoneri** and the streets beyond, sequined mask and souvenir shops have replaced some of the Venetian craft shops, but it's still fun for browsing, and the occasional artisan can be spotted creating glass insects, fashioning a traditional leather mask or making marble-effect paper. At the end of Calle dei Saoneri, turn left, then right into Calle dei Nomboli.

Halfway along, the stunning masks in the window of **Tragicomica** (no. 2800) capture the attention of passers-by. Every one of them is handmade by craftsmen – hence the prices. Masks range from *commedia dell'arte* characters to allegorical masks of the creator's own invention.

CASA GOLDONI

Opposite the shop is **Casa Goldoni** ❾ (Calle dei Nomboli 2794; tel: 041-275 9325; www.museicivicivenezianiit; Thur–Tue Apr–Oct 10am–5pm, Nov–Mar 10am–4pm; charge), birthplace of the great 18th-century dramatist. Carlo Goldoni's plays are known for their wit, and he incorporated aspects of the familiar *commedia dell'arte* into his works, creating a new genre known as the '*opera buffa*' (comic opera).

From here, follow the signs for the vaporetto back to San Tomà.

Above: Goldoni.

Mask-Making Class
Interested in making your own carnival mask? There are several workshops that invite visitors to join a masterclass. Try Ca' Macana in Dorsoduro (www.ca macanacourses.com; tel: 041-277 6142), which runs a 2½-hour course in five different languages every Wednesday and Friday at 3pm.

Commedia dell'Arte

Many of the most distinctive carnival masks and costumes are inspired by characters from the *commedia dell'arte*. The essentially comic genre emerged in 16th-century Italy and featured improvisation, a fast pace and witty regional parodies. The plot was often secondary to the acrobatics, juggling and miming that kept the performance lively. Stock characters based on regional stereotypes appeared in each performance, identified by their mask. Some of the most recognisable characters are: Arlecchino (Harlequin), the witty, clown-like servant from Bergamo; Pantalone, the miserly Venetian merchant; Dottore, the pompous scholar from Bologna; and Colombina, the wily and clever Venetian female counterpart to Arlecchino.

THE RIALTO

To Venetians, the Rialto is not restricted to the graceful bridge, but embraces the district curved around the middle bend of the Grand Canal – a labyrinth of dark alleys and tiny squares centred on its quayside markets.

DISTANCE 1.5km (1 mile)

TIME 2 hours

START Rialto Mercato vaporetto

END Taverna Campiello del Remer (on the opposite bank)

POINTS TO NOTE

Make an early start to see the markets in full swing and watch the barges offloading at the quayside by the Grand Canal. The best days to do this tour are Tuesday to Saturday, when both main markets are functioning.

For centuries the Rialto has been the commercial hub of the city. It was here that the first inhabitants of the lagoon are said to have settled. By the heyday of the Republic it was one of the major financial quarters of Europe – a thriving centre for bankers, brokers and merchants. The Rialto remains a hive of commercial activity. Threading through the maze of alleys is an intoxicating experience, especially in the morning. Ignore the tourist tat in favour of foodstuffs galore and sampling *cichetti* (Venetian snacks) in one of the remaining *bacari* (traditional wine bars).

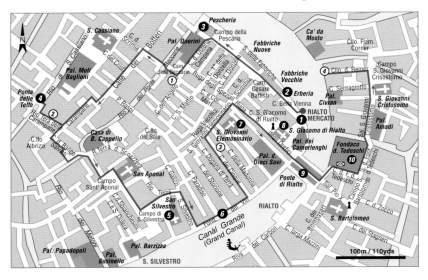

RIALTO MARKETS

This tour commences with a meander through the markets. Set off from the **Rialto Mercato vaporetto ❶** and walk straight ahead into Campo Bella Vienna, a square that bustles with the comings and goings of market shoppers.

Erberia

Turn right onto the Casaria, lined with market stalls and butchers' shops, which will deliver you into the heart of the fruit-and-vegetable market known as the **Erberia ❷**. These stalls create one of the most colourful scenes in Venice, with gleaming peppers and aubergines, thick sticks of asparagus, yellow-flowered courgettes, bags of lemons and bunches of fragrant coriander. With the approach of summer come wild strawberries, plump peaches, cherries, figs and watermelons – all of which eventually make their way onto Venetian dessert menus.

Pescheria

The market extends along the canal banks to the **Pescheria ❸**, the fish market set in an arcaded neo-Gothic hall by the quayside, where gleaming sardines, sole and skate, sea bass and spider crabs, squid and live shrimps are all laid out in trays under the colonnades. Much of the fish and seafood is brought in each day from Chioggia, a fishing town situated on a small island at the southern entrance of the lagoon.

Turn left down Calle Beccarie into Campo delle Beccarie, and, if the mood takes you, join the fishmongers for a morning tipple or a coffee at the **Osteria da Pinto**, see ⑪①.

BEYOND THE RIALTO

Exit the Campo via the wrought-iron bridge in the corner and follow the yellow sign for Ca' Pesaro under the *sottoportego*. Turn left onto Calle dei Botteri, ignoring any yellow signs, and follow the street until it narrows, at which point turn right into the little square marked Carampane. Pass under the *sottoportego*, then take a right into Rio Terà delle Carampane. You are now well off the beaten tourist track. The first bridge on your right is the **Ponte delle Tette ❹** (Bridge of Breasts), named after the prostitutes (of which there were over 11,000 in Venice in the 16th century) who used to frequent this quarter, stripping to the waist to lure their customers into the brothels.

Return to the Rio Terà delle Carampane and stop for a bite to eat at **Antiche Carampane**, see ⑪②.

Food and Drink

① OSTERIA DA PINTO

Campo delle Beccarie; tel: 041-522 4599; Tue–Sun; €€
Although it also offers set menus, this historic Rialto market inn is still popular with locals for tasty snacks (*cichetti*) such as *baccalà mantecato*, salami and bruschetta, all accompanied by simple Veneto wines, sold by the glass.

② ANTICHE CARAMPANE

San Polo 1911; Rio Terà delle Carampane; tel: 041-524 0165; Tue–Sat; €€€
Not easy to find, but worth the search because the seafood dishes are excellent, even if the service can be a bit brusque. You can eat at outside tables in summer.

Traghetti

Before the 19th century, the only way to cross the Grand Canal (other than the Rialto Bridge) was on a *traghetto*, a gondola used exclusively for ferrying passengers from bank to bank. *Traghetti* are still in operation today, connecting the Grand Canal banks at seven strategic points. A journey costs only 50 cents. Venetians normally stand, but feel free to sit if you like.

Below: the Rialto market is a refreshing change from monumental Venice.

SAN SILVESTRO

After lunch, take a right onto Calle Albrizzi, then follow Calle Tamossi left until you reach a canal. Cross the bridge and follow Calle del Ponte Storto into Campo Sant'Aponal. This square may be tiny, but with eight streets leading into it, it is a major crossroads for human traffic. The deconsecrated church of Sant'Aponal is used as an archive. Cross the Campo and head south under the *sottoportego*, which leads into Campo di San Silvestro.

Originally founded in the 12th century, the church of **San Silvestro ❺** (daily 8–11.30am, 3.30–6.30pm; free) was completely rebuilt during the 19th century (the façade was completed in 1909). The highlight of the neo-classical interior is Tintoretto's *Baptism of Christ* (first altar on the right).

Pass in front of the church and turn right into Calle San Silvestro, which leads back to the Grand Canal. Turn left onto the **Fondamenta del Vin ❻**, where barrels of wine used to be unloaded. It is overrun by souvenir stalls and touristy restaurants, but don't be tempted by any of the waiters who might try enticing you to enter. The prices you pay are for the view, not for the quality of the food. Stroll along the canal enjoying the views until you reach Sottoportego dei Cinque. Stop for some refreshment at **Caffè del Doge**, see ⑪③.

SAN GIOVANNI AND SAN GIACOMO

Now continue up Calle dei Cinque, and turn right into San Giovanni Elemosinario, lined with souvenir stalls and teeming with people making their way to the Rialto Bridge. Tucked away behind a metal gate on your right, the church of **San Giovanni Elemosinario ❼** (Mon–Sat 10am–5pm; Chorus Church, *see p.13*; charge) is one of the oldest churches in the area. Pop in here to see Titian's altarpiece *San Giovanni Elemosinario*, a touching portrayal of the saint giving alms; it is characterised by the loose brushstrokes that would mark the artist's later works.

Turn right outside the church, then right again onto Ruga degli Orefici, passing the oldest church in the area, **San Giacomo di Rialto ❽**. Nestling comfortably among the fruit-and-veg-

etable stalls, the church is linked to St James, the patron saint of goldsmiths and pilgrims. Both were much in evidence in the Rialto. Its most distinctive features are the Gothic portico, bell tower and bold 24-hour clock.

Campo San Giacomo preserves its mercantile atmosphere, an echo of Republican times, when money-changers and bankers set up their tables under the church portico. The **Gobbo di Rialto**, the Hunchback of the Rialto, is a curious stooped figure supporting the steps opposite the church: it was on the adjoining pink podium that republican laws were proclaimed, with the burden metaphorically borne by this figure of the Venetian Everyman.

RIALTO BRIDGE

The **Ponte di Rialto** ❾ spans the Grand Canal with a strong, elegantly curved arch of marble, a single-span bridge lined with shops. Until the 1850s, it was the only fixed point for crossing the canal. The current structure is actually the fourth version of the bridge. The first wooden structure was erected in the 14th century, only to be destroyed during a revolt in 1310. A second structure collapsed under the weight of spectators who had gathered to watch the procession for the Marquis of Ferrara in 1444. One can see what the third version looked like by viewing Carpaccio's *Miracle of the True Cross* in the Accademia *(see p.42)*. The current bridge was designed by the appropriately named Antonio da Ponte at the end of the 16th century. The relatively

unknown architect won the commission over giants such as Michelangelo, Sansovino and Palladio, who were all asked to submit designs. Walk along the side aisles, if possible, as they tend to be less crowded than the centre, and afford better views of the palaces, warehouses and water traffic.

THE RIGHT BANK

The building across the bridge and to the left is the **Fondaco dei Tedeschi** ❿, named after the German merchants who once leased the emporium; it is now the city post office. Turn left around the back of the building (away from the sign for San Marco) and cross the bridge into Campo San Giovanni Cristostomo. For a tranquil, truly Venetian dining experience, take the alley on the left, next to the Fiaschetteria Toscana. Follow the street under the *sottoportego* and you will reach the **Taverna di Campiello Remer**, see ⑪④, which offers fine views of the Rialto market.

San Giacomo di Rialto
This is believed to be the oldest church in Venice. Its most distinctive feature is a Gothic 24-hour clock, which dates from 1410; it was restored in the 16th century along with the rest of the building.

Food and Drink

③ CAFFE DEL DOGE

San Polo 609; Calle dei Cinque; tel: 041-522 7787; Mon–Sat; €
A relatively new café, serving 11 different blends of espresso from all over the world. There is also a delicious selection of cakes and fresh juices to choose from.

④ TAVERNA DEL CAMPIELLO REMER

Cannaregio 5701; Campiello del Remer; tel: 041-522 5789; Thur–Tue; €€
This locals' *taverna* can be a bit difficult to find, which is why you will see few tourists here. It serves a good pre-dinner spritz, as well as a variety of wines by the glass. The charming, wood-beamed interior is a lovely setting for sampling classic Venetian dishes, such as *bigoli in salsa* (buckwheat pasta in an anchovy and onion sauce).

CANNAREGIO

Largely residential, Cannaregio is one of the most fascinating but least explored areas of the city. In this half-day tour you visit the world's oldest Ghetto, the peaceful backwaters of the Madonna dell'Orto neighbourhood, and some of the finest Gothic and Renaissance churches in Venice.

Above: Star of David in the Ghetto; Ca' d'Oro.

DISTANCE 3km (2 miles)
TIME 3–4 hours
START Stazione Ferroviaria
END Santa Maria dei Miracoli
POINTS TO NOTE

In summer, this walk is best done early in the morning or late in the afternoon to escape the heat. You might also want to avoid Saturdays, as it's the Sabbath, and most things in the Ghetto are closed. The walk can easily be combined with walk 5 (done backwards) via a short walk to Campo SS Giovanni e Paolo.

Cannaregio is the most densely populated district and the closest to both the railway station and the mainland. It has a neighbourhood feel, with every parish possessing its own church and *campo*. Despite daunting post-war tenements on the fringes of the district, Cannaregio is alive with activity, with the space for chattering children and dozing cats. Glimpses of everyday life on secluded balconies or through half-shuttered blinds reveal elderly Venetians passing the time of day with their neighbours, or leaning out of windows hung with washing. The tangle of alleys reveals the occasional *bottega* selling woodcarvings,

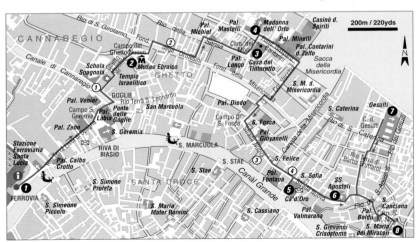

as well as earthy, hole-in-the-wall bars and small *alimentari* (grocery stores), a rarity in more upmarket parts of Venice.

LISTA DI SPAGNA

Start at the **Stazione Ferroviaria S. Lucia ❶** (the train station) and follow the flow along the Lista di Spagna, then take the Ponte delle Guglie (Bridge of the Obelisks) across the Cannaregio Canal. This waterway was the main entrance to the city before the railway bridge was built in 1846 to link the city to the mainland. This is a lively quarter with waterside stalls and a morning market along the Rio Terrà San Leonardo ahead of you.

THE GHETTO

Turn left after the bridge where you see a yellow sign in Hebrew and Italian directing you towards the Synagogue, and take the third covered passageway on your right signposted 'Sinagoghe'. Before heading on, depending on the time of day, you might consider a bite to eat at **Gam-Gam**, see ⑪①.

This passageway, dotted with small shops, galleries and workshops, leads to the **Ghetto Vecchio** (Old Ghetto) and Campiello delle Scuole. Cross the bridge into the **Campo del Ghetto Nuovo** (New Ghetto Square), which, despite the name, stands at the heart of world's oldest ghetto, a fortified island created in 1516. In the early 16th century, Jews in Venice were confined to this island. It became one of the major Jewish communities in Europe with a

population density three times greater than in the most crowded Christian suburb. The only answer to these cramped conditions was to build upwards. Hence the 'skyscrapers' of Venice, tenement blocks of five or six storeys that were once the highest blocks in Europe. The community remained on the site until 1797, when Napoleon had the gates torn down, and from then on Jews had the freedom to live wherever they liked in the city. Today, only a handful of Jewish families still live here, though the area is rich in Jewish culture with restaurants, bakeries, and stores selling Jewish handicrafts.

The most striking feature of the large Campo del Ghetto Nuovo is the series of evocative bas-reliefs recording the Nazi holocaust, by Arbit Blatas. You will see them on the near side of the square, below symbolic strips of barbed wire. Three of Venice's five remaining synagogues are set around the square.

Jewish Museum

The **Museo Ebraico ❷** (Campo del Ghetto Nuovo 2902/A; tel: 041-715 359; www.museoebraico.it; Sun–Fri June–Sept 10.30am–5.30pm, Oct–May 10.30am–3.30pm, Fri until 4.30pm; charge) lies on the opposite side of the square. From here English/Italian

Above from far left: 13th-century figure in the Campo dei Mori; holocaust memorial in the Ghetto Nuovo; Cannaregio's Ponte delle Guglie.

Venetian Dialect
Familiarising yourself with a few geographical terms may help to identify places on your trails through the confusing backwaters: a *fondamenta* is a quayside beside a canal (known as a *rio*); a *sottoportego* is a tiny alleyway running under a building; a *campiello* is a small *campo* (square); a *ruga* is a broad shopping street and a *calle* is an alley. For more details, see p.100.

Food and Drink 🍴

① GAM-GAM
Cannaregio 1122, Ponte delle Guglie; tel: 041-715 284; Mon–Sun noon–3pm, Mon, Thur, Sun 6pm–midnight; €
The only kosher restaurant in Venice, Gam-Gam is a focal point for the Jewish community. Serves Israeli and Italian dishes. Try the €9.50 lunch falafel menu, which includes a range of appetizers.

Below: the Campo dei Mori is named after the turbaned Moors that decorate the façade of the Palazzo Mastelli, near Tintoretto's house.

guided tours of the Spanish, German and Levantine synagogues take place hourly on the half-hour.

Fondamenta degli Ormesini

Take the northern exit from the square, cross the bridge with wrought-iron railings and turn right into the **Fonda menta degli Ormesini**. The quayside is always busy with locals, shopping at grocery or household stores and frequenting small bars and trattorias. The affordable prices and picturesque canalside setting of **Al Timon**, see ⑪②, may tempt you to take a break for a glass of wine and light meal.

TINTORETTO'S NEIGHBOURHOOD

Turn left down the narrow Calle del Forno, marked with a blue 'Istituto Ospedaliero', cross the bridge and turn right into the pretty Fondamenta della Sensa. Follow the canal as far as **Campo dei Mori**. The statues here depict merchants of the Mastelli family, who came to Venice from the Peloponnese in the 12th century.

Tintoretto's House

Beyond the Campo, another turbaned merchant occupies a niche in the wall, just before the **Casa di Tintoretto ❸** (Fondamenta dei Mori 3399). The insignificant-looking building is marked with a plaque and bas-relief of the artist, who lived here with his family from 1574 until his death in 1594. Jacopo Robusti derived his nickname, Tintoretto, from his father's profession of dyer *(tintore)*. He lived his whole life in Cannaregio and only left Venice once.

Towards the Madonna dell'Orto

Return to the Campo dei Mori, cross the bridge on the far side and turn right for views of the relief of a one-legged man and a camel on the canal façade of the Gothic **Palazzo Mastelli**, which adds to the Eastern flavour of this area.

Ajacent to the palace is the lovely **Madonna dell'Orto ❹** (Campo della Madonna dell'Orto; Mon–Sat 10am–5pm; Chorus Church, *see p.13*; charge), a masterpiece of Venetian Gothic, conspicuous for its oriental campanile, richly embellished façade and beautiful

CAMPO DEI MORI

carved portal. Inside it showcases Tintoretto's paintings, some of which are considered his finest outside the Scuola di San Rocco *(see p.65)*. This was the artist's parish church, and he is buried in the chapel to the right of the altar.

Wander around this quiet neighbourhood, where washing flaps in the breeze and cats doze in sunlit squares. This is one of the few areas of Venice where gardens are a feature.

CA' D'ORO

Follow the canal eastwards, crossing the bridge at the end. From here you can catch glimpses across the lagoon of the islands of San Michele *(see below)* and Murano *(see p.79)*. Continue to the end of the street, crossing over three bridges, until you rejoin the bustling flow of the Strada Nova in Campo di S. Fosca. Follow the Strada Nova eastwards to

Above from far left: canal reflections; in the Campo dei Mori.

Below: the Madonna dell'Orto.

Food and Drink

② AL TIMON
Cannaregio 2754, Fondamenta degli Ormesini; tel: 340-244 0245; Tue–Sun; €
A beautiful canalside setting and laid-back atmosphere make this a favourite. The kitchen serves three or four hot dishes a day, plus salads and delicious crostini. Great for a light, informal meal.

③ LA CANTINA
Cannaregio 3689, Campo San Felice; tel: 041-522 8258; Tue–Sat; €€
The owners light up this small establishment, cooking up everything from sandwiches to platters of fresh seafood carpaccio. There is an excellent wine selection by the glass, and the outdoor seating gives the chance for some serious people-watching.

④ ALLA VEDOVA
Cannaregio 3912, Ramo Ca' d'Oro; tel: 041-528 5324; Fri–Wed, closed Sun am; €
This long-running establishment is known for its wine selection and variety of hearty *cicchetti*. It's also possible to have a full meal based on traditional Venetian seafood dishes, but best to book in advance, as it is popular with locals and tourists alike.

San Michele

San Michele, site of the city cemetery, is easily identified from the mainland by its solemn cypress trees. As the island closest to Venice, it is served by ferries from the Fondamente Nuove. Formerly a prison island, it was Napoleon who decreed that the dead should be brought here, away from the crowded city. The rambling cemetery is lined with gardens stacked with simple memorials or domed family mausoleums. Here lie the tombs of dogal families, obscure diplomats and plague victims, along with such illustrious figures as Stravinsky, Ezra Pound and Diaghilev. Famous foreigners are allowed to rest in peace, but more modest souls tend to be evicted – after 10 years their remains are exhumed and placed in permanent storage boxes. By the landing stage, the cemetery's focal point is the cool, austere Renaissance church of San Michele in Isola. A trip to this peaceful and remote spot is haunting and memorable.

Above from left:
intricate ceiling detail in Santa Maria dei Miracoli; the jewel-like Renaissance exterior of Santa Maria dei Miracoli, a favourite for Venetian weddings; Murano is famous for its glass; Burano is the home of fishermen and lacemakers.

Above: the Gesuiti peeking out from between Venetian townhouses; fountain on the Fondamente di Cannaregio.

Venetians' Venice
Cannaregio is the second-largest neighbourhood in Venice (Castello is the biggest), but has the highest population (about 20,000).

the Ca' d'Oro, the next stop. En route, take a break for wine and people-spotting at **La Cantina**, see ⑪③, or *cicchetti* at **Alla Vedova**, see ⑪④, see p.77

The **Ca' d'Oro** ❺, one of the finest palaces on the Grand Canal, is home to the Franchetti Gallery (Calle Ca' d'Oro 3932; tel: 041-522 2349; www.cadoro. org; Mon 8.15am–2pm, Tue–Sun 8.15am–7.15pm; last entrance 30 min before closing; charge), a collection of Renaissance treasures. The most prized piece is Mantegna's *St Sebastian*; Tullio Lombardo's delightful marble *Double Portrait*, inspired by ancient funerary reliefs, is also worth singling out. The *portego* is a showcase of sculpture and opens onto the Grand Canal. The palace interior suffered barbaric restoration in the mid-19th century, but still offers fantastic views of the Grand Canal. Viewing the exterior from the Grand Canal, however, you can see why the Ca' d'Oro is one of the city's great showpieces *(see p.37)*.

Coming out of the Ca' d'Oro, turn right back onto the Strada Nova, which leads to the bustling *campo* and church of **SS Apostoli** ❻ (8am–noon, 5–7pm; free), which contains a painting by Tiepolo and an exquisite marble relief of St Sebastian by Tullio Lombardo.

THE GESUITI

Take the northern exit out of the *campo*, behind the church, and you'll come to a small square. At the end of Calle del Manganer, take a left, crossing two bridges until you reach the **Campo dei Gesuiti**. The large ex-monastery of the

Jesuits on your right, with bricked-up windows, was once used as a barracks and is awaiting restoration.

A little further along is the **Gesuiti** ❼ (10am–noon, 4–6pm; free), a Jesuit church founded in 1714, with no expense spared on its construction: the interior is a riot of gilded stucco and lavishly sculpted green-and-white marble. Titian's *Martyrdom of St Lawrence* hangs in the first altar on the left.

Just north of the church you can enjoy fine lagoon views from the Fondamente Nuove, the wide northern quayside. If the mood strikes and time allows, you can make a detour and visit the cemetery island of San Michele *(see p.77)* by taking the 41 or 42 vaporetto towards Murano for one stop.

SANTA MARIA DEI MIRACOLI

For your final destination, head out of Campo dei Gesuiti the way you came in, walk as far as Calle Muazzo, then follow the signs for Ospedale SS Giovanni e Paolo and Santa Maria dei Miracoli through Campo S. Canzian until you reach Campo S. Maria.

Across the bridge and to the right is the ornate Renaissance church of **Santa Maria dei Miracoli** ❽ (Campo Santa Maria dei Miracoli; Mon–Sat 10am–5pm; Chorus Church, *see p.13*; charge). Rising sheer from the water, the façade offers a dazzling display of marble. Inside, the surfaces are a vision of pale pinks and silvery greys, and pilasters adorned with interlaced flowers, mythical creatures and cavorting mermaids.

MURANO, BURANO
AND TORCELLO

*Spend a day exploring this trio of lagoon islands. Watch glass-blowing in
Murano, wander the brightly coloured banks of Burano, and visit the
surviving sights of Torcello, once the principal settlement of Venice.*

This tour takes you away from central
Venice, incorporating several vaporetto
trips, a look into the historic Venetian
crafts of glass-making and lace, and a
visit to the city's former epicentre.

MURANO

The island of Murano is sometimes
described as a mini-Venice. It cannot
match the city for splendour but, like
Venice, it is made up of islands and
divided by canals, which are lined with
old mansions and *palazzi*. It even has
its own Grand Canal. But Murano's
raison d'être is – and has been for centuries – the making of glass. As early
as the 7th century a glass industry was
established near Venice. In the late
13th century the factories were moved
to Murano to avoid the hazards of fire
from the open furnaces. The Murano
glass-makers enjoyed rare privileges.
But their craft was a closely guarded
secret, and the makers left the shores
of Venice on pain of death. Even so,
many of them were lured abroad in the
16th century. Those who were discovered, including a few who divulged
their secrets to the court of Louis XIV,
were condemned to death. Today
about 60 percent of the glass produced

> **DISTANCE** 5km (3¼ miles)
> **TIME** A full day
> **START** Museo vaporetto, Murano
> **END** Museo dell'Estuario, Torcello
> **POINTS TO NOTE**
> It's best to have a vaporetto pass for
> this excursion, as you will need to
> use several different boats. To reach
> the starting point above, take a
> vaporetto from Fondamente Nuove
> or San Zaccaria. Try to avoid week-
> ends, when the islands are packed
> with tourists. Beware of free trips to
> Murano offered by touts near Piazza
> San Marco – for each tourist brought
> to a showroom, the tout is paid a
> hefty commission, hence the pres-
> sure to buy and the elevated prices.

**Navigating
the Lagoon**
Many sections
of the lagoon are
unnavigable because
of the mudflats and
sandbanks, but
skilled boatmen can
weave through the
shifting channels
and sandbars,
guided by the
bricole – distinctive
navigational markers.

on Murano is exported. The character-
istics of the local glass are deep, bright
colours and ornate design.

It's easy to get to the island independently: vaporetti 41 and 42 depart from
Fondamente Nuove in Cannaregio or
the San Zaccaria landing in San Marco.
(Both vaporetti also stop at the island of
San Michele – *see p.77*). To avoid the
pressure from smooth-operating glass
vendors, wait until the **Museo stop** ❶

on Murano before you get off. Signs will lead you to the **Museo del Vetro ❷** (Glass Museum, Fondamenta Giustinian 8; tel: 041-739 586; www.museicivicivineziani.it; Thur–Tue 10am–6pm, winter until 5pm; charge), containing a stunning collection of Venetian glass. A prize piece is the Coppa Barovier (Barovier being one of a dynasty of Muranese glass-makers) – a 15th-century wedding chalice adorned with allegorical love scenes.

SS Maria e Donato

Leaving the museum, turn left and follow Fondamenta Giustinian for the basilica of **SS Maria e Donato ❸** (Campo San Donato; 9am–noon, 4–7pm, closed Sun am; free). Founded in the 7th century and remodelled in the Veneto-Byzantine style, it is the finest church on Murano. Despite heavy-handed restoration, it retains

some outstanding features: the colonnaded apse exterior on the canalside, with its wonderful decorative brick exterior, the 12th-century mosaic *pavimento* with medieval motifs and symbolic animals, the ship's keel roof and the mosaic of the Madonna and Child over the apse.

Fondamenta Longa

Retrace your steps to the Museo landing stage, follow the Fondamenta Longa along Murano's own Canal Grande and cross the Ponte Vivarini (sometimes called Ponte Longo) – named after the 15th-century family of painters who lived on Murano. From the bridge you can see the **Palazzo da Mula** (on the far bank to your right), one of Murano's few surviving grand mansions.

Fondamenta dei Vetrai

Across the bridge and to the left is the Gothic church of **San Pietro Martire ❹** (Fondamenta dei Vetrai; 9am–noon, 3–6pm, closed Sun am; free) housing two fine altarpieces by Giovanni Bellini. The interior also contains spec-

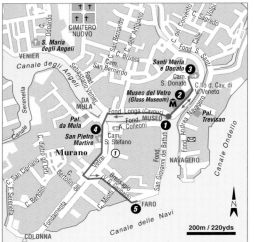

tacular Murano glass chandeliers and bottle-glass windows in lovely hues. If you are feeling hungry, cross the canal via the bridge directly in front of the church into Campo Santo Stefano, and enjoy a meal at **Trattoria Busa alla Torre**, see ⑪①.

After lunch, amble along the Fondamenta dei Vetrai, the heart of the glass-making district. The glass factories and showrooms along the quayside offer a chance to admire the glass-blowers' skills. In the morning, market boats selling fresh produce along the canal add to the busy scene. If you haven't yet seen a glass-blowing display, let yourself be lured into one of the workshops (there should be no obligation to buy, though you might receive a sales pitch). With incredible skill the maestro blows the blob of molten glass, then with a spatula and a pair of pincers, twists, turns, pinches and flattens it into the perfect shape of an animal or bird. If you are tempted to pick up a souvenir from one of the glass shops, do beware of imitations from the Far East *(see margin, p.80)*.

To continue on to Burano, cross the canal at Ponte de Mezo and take Viale Bressagio across the square. This leads to the **Murano Faro stop ❺**, where you can catch vaporetto LN for the 30-minute ride to Burano.

BURANO

This most vibrant of Venetian islands makes a cheery stop en route to Torcello, its polar opposite. Once a flourishing centre of the lagoon, it is now a backwater of orchards and gardens with

Above from far left: canal scene in Murano; Venetian glass; exterior of SS Maria e Donato.

Below left: symbol of the island. **Below:** colourful building and boat in Burano.

a Romanesque/Gothic church, some simple dwellings and a couple of trattorias. About 5,000 people live here, many of them fishermen or glass-workers who commute to the factories of Murano.

From the **landing stage ⑥**, follow the general flow down via Marcello, past souvenir stalls and brightly painted houses. Turn left at the end of the street and cross over the bridge, turning left again onto the Fondamenta dei Assassini. To view the most colourful *cortile* (courtyard) on the island, take the tiny alley marked Via al Gattolo. At no. 339, **Casa Bepi ⑦** has a dazzling multicoloured, geometrical façade.

If you are planning to eat, continue on to Via Baldassare Galuppi, the main street, named after the composer who was born here. Try either the **Trattoria da Romano**, see ⑪②, an ex-haunt of artists, or **Osteria ai Pescatori**, see ⑪③. Stick to fish – either in soup, risotto, pasta or freshly fried or grilled – and you are unlikely to be disappointed.

Lace and Linen

The lace and linen stalls and shops on the island all vie for attention. There are some reasonable purchases to be had among the tablecloths, napkins and blouses, but don't be fooled into thinking it is all handmade on Burano; virtually all of it is factory-made in Asia. Also note that the prices on the island are the same as those in Venice itself.

The downfall of the Republic led to the inevitable decline of the lace industry, but a revival took place in 1872 when a lacemaking school was founded in an effort to combat local poverty. Today Burano is one of the last surviving centres of handmade lace.

Museo del Merletto

To see authentic Burano lace and the ladies who make it, visit the **Museo del Merletto ⑧** (Lace Museum; Piazza Galuppi; tel: 041-730 034; www.musei civiciveneziani.it; Wed–Mon 10am–5pm, until 4pm in winter; charge). Here priceless antique pieces are displayed behind glass, and upstairs the women busily knit away in the old tradition.

Retrace your steps to the vaporetto landing to continue the journey to Torcello, a short jaunt from Burano on Line T, which departs every half-hour.

Food and Drink

② DA ROMANO
Burano, Via Galuppi 221; tel: 041-730 030; Wed–Mon, closed Sun dinner; €€
A long-established restaurant set in the island's former lace school. The interior is lit by glass lamps and adorned with paintings donated by visiting artists.

③ OSTERIA AI PESCATORI
Burano, Piazza Galuppi 371; tel: 041-730 650; Thur–Tue; €€€
This welcoming restaurant serves fish and game. Try the seafood risotto or tagliolini with cuttlefish *(seppie)*.

④ LOCANDA CIPRIANI
Torcello, Piazza Santa Fosca 29; tel: 041-730 150; Feb–Dec Wed–Mon lunch; €€€€
This remote but lovely inn run by the nephew of Arrigo Cipriani, the owner of Harry's Bar, is a local institution. Try the grilled fish, fillet steak or risotto alla torcellana. Book in advance.

⑤ AL PONTE DEL DIAVOLO
Torcello, Fondamenta Borgognoni 10; tel: 041-730 401; Mar–Dec Tue–Sun; €€€
A great atmosphere and efficient service in this pleasant rustic lunch venue. Pasta and seafood are specialities. Lunch only, though dinner can be reserved for special events.

TORCELLO

It is hard to believe that this flat little island, whose inhabitants now number only around 70, was once the centre of a thriving civilisation. In its heyday, Torcello's population was around 20,000, but, as Venice rose to power, decline set in. Trade dwindled and the waters silted up and spread. Today the cathedral, church and a couple of *palazzi* are the sole evidence of former splendour. It is a lonely, nostalgic and, if you are in the mood, romantic island.

From the **landing stage ❾**, where you can spot the cathedral bell tower rising above the flat marshland, follow the rustic path beside a narrow canal. It all seems extraordinarily quiet and rural in comparison with the city.

If you arrive at lunchtime, options include the **Locanda Cipriani**, see ⑪④, where you will be following in the footsteps of Hemingway, Queen Elizabeth II, Sir Winston Churchill, Charlie Chaplin and Sophia Loren, to name a few. A less pricey alternative

is the pleasantly rural **Al Ponte del Diavolo**, see ⑪⑤.

Santa Maria dell'Assunta

After lunch, carry on down the same rustic path and start your sightseeing where the settlement began: the cathedral of **Santa Maria dell'Assunta ❿** (Piazza di Torcello; Mar–Oct daily 10am–6pm, Nov–Feb until 5pm; charge, a combined ticket is available for the cathedral, campanile and museum). The oldest church in Venice, it was founded in AD639 but rebuilt between the 9th and 11th centuries. Note the foundations of the original baptistery on your left as you enter and the massive, 11th-century stone slabs acting as shutters on the south side of the cathedral.

The interior is impressive, and its lovely mosaics are among the oldest and finest in Italy. Most striking of all is *The Virgin and Child*, set against a glowing gold background in the dome of the central apse. Covering the western wall is *The Last Judgement*, a

Burano Lace

In the 16th century, Venetian, and particularly Burano, lace was in great demand, so much so that the court of Louis XIV closed its doors to lace from Venice and created a royal industry of its own. Every means possible was used to steal the industry from La Serenissima, by inducing women to leave Burano and providing them with workshops where new designs – though clearly Venetian in influence – were invented.

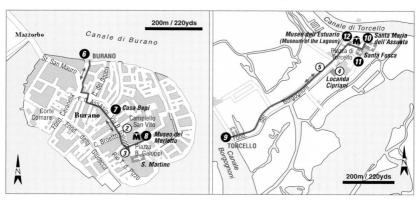

Above from left:
tranquil scene in
the lagoon; the Lido.

massive mosaic full of narrative. From this end admire the church in its entirety: the slender marble columns, the wooden tie-beams and the rood-screen carved with peacocks, lions and flowers, surmounted by a frieze of 15th-century paintings. Afterwards, climb up the campanile for fine views of the lagoon.

Other Highlights

The church of **Santa Fosca** ⓫, which adjoins the cathedral via a pretty portico, was built in the 11th century to enshrine the body of Santa Fosca, the Christian martyr. Close to the church, the primitive stone chair known as **Attila's Seat** was once said to have been used by the king of the Huns. A more likely theory is that it was used by the island tribunes. According to local folklore, if you sit on the chair you will be married within the year. On the opposite side of the piazza, the **Museo dell' Estuario** ⓬ (Estuary Museum; daily Mar–Oct 10.30am–5.30pm, Nov–Feb 10am– 5pm; charge) contains archaeological finds from the earliest days of the island's history.

Ferries go from Burano back to Venice until late at night, and one or two go direct from Torcello. Dusk, when the sun is setting over the lagoon, is a beautiful time to return.

Smaller Islands

As your boat takes you through the northern lagoon, past Murano, and on towards Burano and Torcello, you will pass a number of small islands. On your right for most of the journey from Murano to Burano, you can see the marshy islets and main island of Sant'Erasmo, where fruit and vegetables are grown for Venetian consumption. First, however, you will pass Le Vignole, an island where, during the summer, many Venetians stop to swim and eat at the delicious rustic restaurant located here (Alle Vignole; Apr–Sept Tue–Sun). Both Le Vignole and Sant'Erasmo are accessible by vaporetto 13 from the Fondamente Nuove. Service is sporadic, so you'll want to check the schedules. The ferry swings left around the deserted island of San Giacomo in Palude, one of many abandoned in the 1960s. To the right, in the distance a dark cluster of cypresses marks the romantic island of San Francesco del Deserto, where St Francis is said to have retreated in 1220. The island is not accessible by public transport, so in order to arrive, you will need to hire a boat from one of the local fishermen on Burano. The monastery has recently been renovated, and the Franciscan friars offer guided visits (tel: 041-528 6863; www.isola-sanfrancescodel deserto.it; Tue–Sun 9–11am, 3–5pm; free). Sant'Erasmo and San Francesco del Deserto are agricultural islands, especially known for asparagus and artichokes. Their fresh produce is brought in daily to the markets at the Rialto.

THE LIDO

Leave the sights of the city, catch a vaporetto to Venice's main bathing resort and cool off in the waters of the Adriatic, enjoy its Belle Epoque architecture and maybe go for a gentle cycle ride along the sea wall.

The long strip of land, around 11km (7 miles), protecting the Venetian lagoon from the Adriatic Sea, was Italy's first lido. In the 19th century, when it was no more than a spit of sand, Byron, Shelley and other Romantics came to escape the city, riding along its white sands and bathing in its waters. By the turn of the 20th century it was one of the most fashionable resorts in Europe, and the name was subsequently applied to dozens of bathing resorts throughout the world. The Lido may have lost its cachet since *Death in Venice* was set here, but the beach still provides an essential cooling-off experience on a scorching hot day. The ferry ride across the lagoon, which only takes 12 to 15 minutes, is fun in itself.

DISTANCE 6km (4 miles)

TIME A full day

START Piazzale Santa Maria Elisabetta

END Grand Hotel Excelsior

POINTS TO NOTE

Unless you are affluent enough to go by gondola or motor launch, take a no. 1, 2, 51 (summer only) or LN from the Riva degli Schiavoni (no. 1, 2, 51, and 61 also go from the Piazzale Roma) to reach the starting point above. Public boats linking the Lido to the city leave about every four minutes. If you are with children, a trip here will be top priority. Avoid going on Sundays in summer, when all the Venetians flock here.

Bike Rental

As you'll be covering quite a distance, you might consider renting a bike for the day. Try Gardin Anna Valli (Piazzale S.M. Elisabetta 2A; tel: 041-760 005) or Lido on Bike (Gran Viale S.M. Elisabetta 21; tel: 041-526 8019). Bike rental should normally cost between €10 and €15 a day.

JEWISH CEMETERY AND SAN NICOLÒ

All the ferries arrive on the Lido at the **Piazzale Santa Maria Elisabetta ❶**. Cars, buses and taxis come as something of a shock if you have already acclimatised yourself to the traffic-free streets of Venice. From here, you can take a bus, taxi, hire a bike or go by foot to the eastern side of the island via the **Riviera Santa Maria Elisabetta**. The first landmark of note is the Tempio Votivo, a circular building constructed

in 1925 to commemorate victims of the two world wars. Many of the houses that line this seafront stretch were built in the 1920s, and reflect the fashion for reinterpreting Byzantine and Gothic Venetian architecture.

Jewish Cemetery

Further along the seafront (after it becomes Riviera San Nicolò) is the **Antico Cimitero Ebraico ❷** (Old Jewish Cemetery; entrance on Via Cipro; tel: 041-715 5359; www.museo

Bird's-Eye View

The Lido is Venice's main centre for sport, including water sports, riding, tennis and golf. If you would rather take to the skies, the Aeroclub di Venezia (tel: 041-526 0808) at San Nicolò airport offers hour-long flights over Venice.

ebraico.it; Apr–Sept with guided tours in English every 2nd and 4th Sunday at 3.30pm; charge; call in advance). The Jewish community was granted use of this land in 1386, which reflects the status of Jews in Venice at the time – segregated even in death, they were rowed down the Canale deglie Ebrei to the Lido, the cemetery for outcasts.

San Nicolò

Continuing further along the lagoon shore, you will reach the church and Benedictine monastery of **San Nicolò** ❸ (Piazzale San Nicolò; 9am–noon, 4–7pm; free). From the church there are good views of the **Fortezza di Sant'** **Andrea**, a huge bastion on the island of Le Vignole built between 1535 and 1549 to guard the main entrance of the lagoon. Once a year, the doge would attend Mass at San Nicolò after the annual Marriage of the Sea ritual in the Porto di Lido. From the ceremonial stage barge he would cast a gold ring into the water, symbolising the marriage of Venice with the sea.

When you've finished looking around the church, head back in the direction of the Jewish Cemetery, then turn left down via Giannantonio Selva, which leads to Piazzale Ravà and the beach. A good lunch stop here is **Beer-bante**, see ⑪①.

Food and Drink

① BEERBANTE

Lido di Venezia, Piazzale Ravà 12; tel: 041-526 2550; closed Mon pm, open Fri–Sun in winter; €€
Enjoy heaps of delicious grilled fish and meat at this laid-back beachside bar. This used to be a nightclub, making it a large and spacious atmosphere for dining.

② LIBERTY RESTAURANT

Hôtel des Bains, Lungomare Marconi 17; tel: 041-526 5921; €€
This Art Deco restaurant, decorated with classical frescoes and Murano glass chandeliers, is perfectly pleasant, but the opulent setting is more impressive than the food. There is an additional beach restaurant as well as buffets and snacks served around the pool.

THE SEASIDE

The beach directly in front of Piazzale Ravà forms part of the public, therefore free, beach. However, being free, it's an area that is inevitably less desirable. Following the beach west will take you past the controversial new **Blue Moon** complex. Named after a nightclub that stood here in the Dolce Vita days, this is a hub of activity by night, and provides terraces and a sea-view restaurant and bar by day.

Lungomare G. Marconi

Shortly after the Blue Moon, you come to the **Lungomare G. Marconi**, the boulevard with the best hotels and beaches. You can treat yourself to one of the striped *cabanas* with comfortable sunbeds provided by hotels, but these do not come cheap. You cannot do much better than the beach opposite the Hôtel des Bains *(see below)*, where the sand is manicured daily. Otherwise, keep to the sand nearest to the water's edge, where no one can turf you off. Dubious Italian surveys have found the waters at the Lido to be among the cleanest along the Adriatic coast. Judge for yourself.

Hôtel des Bains

The **Hôtel des Bains** ❹ *(see p.115)* is the Lido's most famous landmark, immortalised by Thomas Mann in his 1912 novella *Death in Venice*. The book tells of Gustav von Aschenbach, an author with writer's block who comes to Venice for a restorative stay; but the lagoon's heady, claustrophobic, muggy setting sparks a mid-life crisis, when von Aschenbach falls in love with a Polish boy also staying at the hotel; Italian director Luchino Visconti's 1971 screen adaptation, starring Dirk Bogarte and filmed on the Lido, brought the novella to a wider audience. If you wish to relive scenes from the film, dine at the hotel's **Liberty Restaurant**, see ⑪②.

Lido Palazzi

Further along the seafront, the former **Palazzo del Casinò** (now a congress centre) and the **Palazzo della Mostra del Cinema** ❺ are typical of the Fascist architecture of the 1930s. In late August/early September celebrities flock to the latter for the Film Festival *(see p.23 and below)*.

End your trip admiring the exuberant late 19th- to early 20th-century neo-Byzantine **Excelsior Hotel** ❻.

Above from far left: beach huts *(cabanas)* on the beach at the Lido; the Liberty Restaurant at the Hôtel des Bains.

Venice Film Festival

Venice is the world's oldest film festival and now rivals Cannes in prestige and the Côte d'Azur in terms of glitz. Early on, the festival celebrated such vintage performances as Greta Garbo in *Anna Karenina* (1935) and Laurence Olivier's *Hamlet* (1948), while directors of the calibre of John Ford and Auguste Renoir brought glamour to the Lido. The glory days coincided with New Wave cinema in the 1960s, a fame sealed by the movies of Godard, Pasolini, Tarkovsky and Visconti. Recently, the festival has gone all out for Hollywood glitz, and big names still get top billing, even if worthy art-house winners tend to triumph in the end. The opening film in 2008 was the Coen Brothers' *Burn After Reading* with an all-star cast including George Clooney and Brad Pitt, but the winner of the coveted Golden Lion (Leon d'Oro) award for Best Film went to *The Wrestler* by New York film-maker Darren Aronofsky.

VENICE IN A DAY

Around 7 million people a year (about half the city's visitors) are daytrippers. If you are among this number and want to do a whistle-stop tour, follow this route, which pulls together highlights from many of the other walks.

Above: on the Grand Canal; Rialto Bridge.

Extending the Tour
Have more time? You can always add a more in-depth exploration of southern Dorsoduro *(see walk 7, p.57)* or head back towards San Rocco and take in the church of the Frari and the San Polo district *(see walk 9, p.65).*

DISTANCE 3km (2 miles)
TIME A full day
START/END Stazione Ferroviaria Santa Lucia
POINTS TO NOTE

This walk is designed to last from 9am to 5pm, allowing time for meals and snacks. If you are travelling to and from Venice by train, remember to leave plenty of time to arrive back at the train station – it is a 30-minute vaporetto ride from San Toma back to the station via vaporetto no. 1, or 15 minutes via vaporetto no. 2, for example. It is also a good idea to buy a 12-hour vaporetto ticket (€14), since you will be using this mode of transport several times during your day. Note that this day can easily start at Piazzale Roma, where you can catch the no. 1 vaporetto. Wear sensible shoes, and sunscreen in the summer. Those looking to condense the day due to time constraints should travel via vaporetto no. 2, which makes fewer stops.

Though one can only scratch the surface of Venice's immense artistic, cultural, and social history in one day, this walk will find you spending a morning in the grand Piazza San Marco with an afternoon in a lively square that is popular with a local crowd. This mix aims to whet your appetite for Venice and make you thirst for a return visit.

GRAND CANAL AND RIALTO

Start at the **Stazione Ferroviaria Santa Lucia** ❶ (Venice's train station), taking either the no. 1 vaporetto on the 13-minute ride to the Rialto Mercato stop. Take in the fantastic architecture found along the Grand Canal, paying particular note of the ornately Gothic Ca' d'Oro *(see p.37 and p.77).*

Rialto Markets
Disembark at **Rialto Mercato** ❷, walk straight ahead into Campo Bella Vienna, and, if you are arriving on any day other than Sunday, drink in the sites, smells, and sounds of the famous Rialto market *(see p.70).* The Rialto, the first area in Venice to be populated, has long been the commercial heart of the lagoon.

First, turn left and take the time to wander through the Erberia as well, with its canalside bars *(see p.71),* which is a pleasant stop for photographs. Heading back into Campo Bella

Vienna, turn right onto the Casaria, which will take you through the produce stalls and toward the two covered **Pescheria ❸** (Fish Market; Tue–Sat; *see p.71*). The market makes a nice place to stock up on snacks for the next leg of your trip.

From the Pescheria, take any of the streets on your left and then head south down the Ruga degli Speziali, the street of the spice traders, where you may catch a whiff of fresh coffee beans and the spices that are still sold from a couple of grocery stores. If you are looking to have a coffee or perhaps snack on some traditional *cichetti* (the Venetian version of tapas; *see p.16*), wander over to the tiny **All'Arco**, see ①, a great place for a pitstop

Rialto Bridge

Returning to the Ruga degli Speziali, continue south down the Ruga dei

Orefici, past the church of San Giacomo di Rialto (the oldest church in Venice; *see p.72*), and over the **Ponte di Rialto ❹** (*Rialto Bridge; see p.73*). The bridge remained the only permanent crossing point on the Grand Canal until the 19th century, making it an important location for merchants.

Fondaco dei Tedeschi

Straight ahead, the building slightly to the left is the **Fondaco dei Tedeschi ❺** (*see p.73*), now the central post office. At one time the Germans used

Above from far left: gondolas on the waterfront near the Piazza San Marco; a modern interpretation of the traditional *bacaro (see p.16)*, in *Sestiere* San Marco.

Food and Drink

① ALL'ARCO

San Polo 436, Calle dell'Occhialer; tel: 041-520 5666; Mon–Sat; €

This impossibly small *osteria* sets out a few tables, which are invariably fought over by the regular customers as well as tourists in the know. The friendly owners serve some of the best *cichetti* in town, as well as sandwiches and crostini.

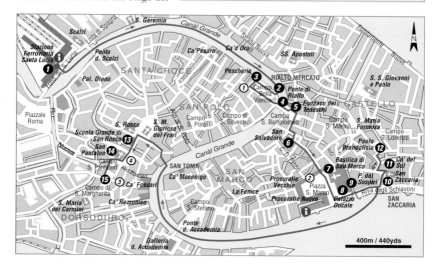

Lunch Early
When planning when
to stop for lunch,
make sure you don't
wait too long.
Many of the smaller
restaurants close
between lunch and
dinner sittings, so you
just might be shut out.

Above: sculpture
of Adam on the
Palazzo Ducale;
Bridge of Sighs.

this building as their warehouse, mercantile offices and as lodging for Germans trading in the lagoon.

SAN MARCO

Coming straight off the bridge down Salizzada Pio X brings you to the San Marco district *(see p.28 and p.46)*, most famous for its Piazza, but also containing many other fine attractions.

San Salvadore

Turn right down the Marzarietta (also known as via 2 Aprile), until you arrive at the church of **San Salvadore** ❻ (Campo San Salvadore; Mon–Sat 9am–noon, 3–6pm, Sun 3–7pm; free). The church, built in the 16th century, contains two lovely works by Titian, an *Annunciation,* located in the third altar to the left, and *The Transfiguration,* at the high altar. The tomb of Caterina Cornaro, queen of Cyprus, can be found in the south transept. Caterina's fate outlines the use of marriage as a political pawn in Venetian history. As a young girl she was married to the king of Cyprus, a move made to seal

---

Food and Drink 🍴
② CAFFÈ QUADRI
Procuratie Vecchie, Piazza San
Marco; tel: 041-522 2105; daily,
Tue–Sun in winter; €€€
In addition to the famous bar,
this is the only proper restaurant on
the Piazza, serving Venetian dishes
as well as creative twists on classic
Italian cuisine. The seafood grill and
risotto are recommended. Booking
is essential.

---

the links between Venice and the country. When her husband died in 1474 – some say at the design of the Venetians – she inherited his kingdom. She was eventually 'persuaded' by Venice to cede Cyprus, and, in exchange, she was given the small Veneto town of Asolo.

Coming out of the church, take the Mercerie S. Salvadore south, continuing on until you enter Piazza San Marco under the Torre dell'Orologio *(see p.35)*.

Piazza San Marco

You have now arrived in what is the only square worthy of the title piazza in Venice. Napoleon called it 'the most elegant drawing room in Europe', although this does make one wonder why he then proceeded to hack down one end of it – now the site of the Ala Napoleonica (Napoleonic Wing) – destroying in the process Sansovino's church of San Geminiano.

If you have some time, you could enjoy a spritz, a traditional aperitif made of campari or aperol and prosecco, at one of the cafes on the square, such as **Caffè Quadri**, see 🍴②, or its rival, **Caffè Florian** *(see p.29)*.

Basilica San Marco

Next stop is the **Basilica San Marco** ❼ (Piazza San Marco; tel: 041-522 5205; daily 9.45am–4.45pm; charge only for Museo Marciano, Pala d'Oro and Treasury; *see p.28*). To maximise your time, reserve tickets in advance with Alata (www.alata.it). Alternatively, and if you

have luggage, you can check your bags in at the nearby Ateneo Basso (just off Piazzetta Leoncina on Calle San Basso), and you will be given a tag that allows you to skip the queue.

Once the private chapel of the Venetian doge, the basilica is decorated to impress. Visits last only about 10 minutes, as you are shuffled along a roped-off route, but you will still have time to take in the impressive mosaic interior. Make sure you pop into the Museo Marciano, where you can view the bronze horses originally brought back from Constantinople to crown the main door of the basilica (the ones currently outside are copies), as well as fantastic views over the square.

Palazzo Ducale

While you don't really have time on this tour to go into the **Palazzo Ducale** ❽ *(see p.32)*, you can, of course, still admire the gloriously Gothic façade, where white stone and pink marble are used to dazzling effect. If you have time, take a closer look at some of the column capitals that ring the building. In the left-hand corner, closest to the Basilica San Marco, is a depiction of the Judgement of Solomon. Other capitals depict professions, animals and goods that were typical in the Republic of Venice, all showing the use of architecture to promote civic glory.

Exit the square in the direction of the lagoon, passing two columns topped by San Teodoro, the former patron saint of Venice, and the Winged Lion, the symbol of St Mark, the current patron saint of the city.

The Molo and Bridge of Sighs

Turn left onto the quayside, known as the Molo, and standing on the crowded Ponte della Paglia, you will catch a glimpse of the **Ponte dei Sospiri** ❾ (Bridge of Sighs; *see p.34*), constructed to transport criminals from the prisons to the adjoining law courts.

While strolling east along the Molo, the waterfront closest to the Basilica, look out to the lagoon for views of San Giorgio Maggiore *(see p.62)*.

Above from far left: gilded mosaic in the Basilica San Marco; the Molo and the columns of San Marco and San Teodoro, which marked the sea entrance to Venice.

Below: the Basilica San Marco, with the Palazzo Ducale just to the right.

CASTELLO

After passing over the Ponte del Vin, duck under the second *sottoportego* on your left and you will soon find yourself in Campo San Zaccaria. You are now in the Castello area *(see p.50)*, the largest of the city's *sestiere*. Beyond the busy waterfront Riva degli Schiavoni, the district is a good place to experience everyday Venetian life, with dark alleys opening into bright squares, pretty canals and some of the most impressive churches in the city.

Above: interior of the Ca' del Sol mask workshop, on the Fondamenta dell'Osmarin.

Below: the Riva degli Schiavoni, the waterfront southeast of Piazza San Marco.

San Zaccaria

A large part of the land here was once owned by the convent of San Zaccaria, a nunnery that took in the most elite women in Venetian society, even sisters of the doge, often against their will. Take

a quick look into the church of **San Zaccaria** ❿ (Mon–Sat 10am–noon, 4–6pm, Sun 4–6pm; charge; *see p.50)*, especially to view the breathtaking *Sacra Conversazione* by Giovanni Bellini, in the first altar on the left.

Mask–Makers

One cannot appreciate Venice without also appreciating the strong history of craftsmanship in the city. Leave the square by the archway in the northern corner, turn right into Campo San Provolo, under a *sottoportego*, and you will arrive at the Fondamenta dell'Osmarin. On the right you will see **Ca' del Sol** ⓫, at no. 4964. This mask workshop carries on the long-standing tradition of hand-crafting papier mâché masks, often based on characters from the *commedia dell'arte (see p.69)*. The idea of anonymity created by the masks appealed to the Venetians, especially during carnival, since it allowed classes to mingle freely.

Gondola Workshops

Just across the street, down the narrow Calle Corte Rota, you will find the workshop of **Paolo Brandolisio** ⓬ (no. 4725). Paolo is a *remèri*, the name for an artisan who creates *forcole* (the sculptural oarlock necessary for rowing gondolas) and oars. This is one of just four Venetian workshops that produce this part of the gondola. The *forcola* is formed from an aged trunk of wood, and its finely sculptured shape allows for the correct movement of the oar. Don't expect a tour here, but you can certainly watch from the doorway; if you catch

the artisans during downtime, they may be happy to answer questions.

At this point, retrace your steps back to the Molo, then walk slightly east, along the Riva degli Sciavoni. From here, catch the no. 1 or 2 vaporetto from the **San Zaccaria** back up the Grand Canal to the **San Tomà stop**, enjoying the scenery along the way *(see p.36)*.

SAN POLO

The vaporetto deposits you in the San Polo district, which curves into the left bank of the Grand Canal. It is home to two of the city's greatest sights: the Frari, a huge Franciscan church containing maserpieces by Titian and Bellini, and the Scuola di San Rocco, which we visit next.

Scuola Grande di San Rocco

From the vaporetto landing, go straight ahead and turn right into Campo San Tomà. Follow the signs out of the square for Tintoretto's masterpiece, the **Scuola Grande di San Rocco** ⓭ (Salizzada San Rocco; tel: 041-523 4864; www.scuolagrandesanrocco.it; daily Apr–Oct 9am–5.30pm, Nov–Mar 10am–5pm; charge; *see p.65)*.

DORSODURO

The remainder of this tour will mostly be spent exploring the western part of the artistic Dorsoduro neighbourhood, fuelled by the infusion of students at the Ca' Foscari University.

Take the Calle Fianco della Scuola beside the Scuola, then cross the bridge

and at the end turn left and immediately right into Calle San Pantalon; this brings you into the square of the same name. **San Pantalon** ⓮ (Campo San Pantalon; Mon–Sat 8–10am, 4–6pm; free) has a huge ceiling fresco by Fumiani. On the left-hand side of the square, close to the canal, note the old slab that lists varieties of fish and the minimum sizes they had to reach before they were allowed to be sold.

Campo di Santa Margherita

Cross the bridge over the Rio Foscari and walk to the **Campo di Santa Margherita** ⓯, a rectangular 'square' bustling with local life. A good spot to relax after an intense day of walking is **Ai Do Draghi**, see ⑪③, right on the square, or **Arca**, see ⑪④, which is back towards San Pantalon.

Once you've had a chance to rest your weary feet and enjoy a spot of people-watching – this area is usually very lively with locals – retrace your steps to the San Tomà vaporetto. To reach the train station by boat from here, allow yourself approximately 30 to 40 minutes.

Above from far left: window of the Ca' del Sol mask workshop, in Castello; Dorsoduro backstreet and canal.

Food and Drink

③ AI DO DRAGHI
Dorsoduro 3665, Campo Santa Margherita; tel: 041-528 9731; daily winter Fri–Wed; €
Great small bar on the square. Serves a delicious spritz, tasty *tramezzini* made with brie and speck, and good wine.

④ ARCA
Dorsoduro 3757, Calle Lunga San Pantalon; tel: 041-524 2236; Mon–Sat until midnight; €€
Arca combines a main trattoria and pizzeria and an excellent *cichetteria* out front. Popular with local university students.

DIRECTORY

A user-friendly alphabetical listing of practical information, plus hand-picked hotels and restaurants to suit all budgets and tastes, and the lowdown on nightlife.

A

AGE RESTRICTIONS

While there is no law limiting the age for drinking alcohol in Italy, there is a law for serving minors under 16 alcohol in public places such as restaurants and bars. The legal driving age in Italy is 18, though teenagers aged 14 and over are allowed to drive scooters. In Italy one can be married with parental consent at 16 and without at age 18.

B

BUDGETING FOR YOUR TRIP

To give an idea of what to expect cost-wise, here is a list of approximate prices in euros (€). Note that services marked with an asterisk are fixed by the Venetian authorities; check these in *Un Ospite di Venezia (see p.101).*

Airport Transfer from Marco Polo. *By road*: public bus (ACTV) €1.10; airport bus (ATVO) €3; taxi €35 (for up to four people). *By water*: Alilaguna public water launch €12 per person; private water taxi approximately €135 for four people and luggage.

Entertainment. A concert in a main church costs from €25; Fenice opera tickets from €80. Casino admission €5.

Gondolas. The official daytime rate is €80 for 40 mins (up to six people), then €40 for each subsequent 20 mins. The evening rate (from 8pm–8am) is €100. Serenaded gondola tours (40 mins) are €44 per person.

Guided Tours. For a walking tour, allow around €25.

Food. *Tramezzini* (half sandwiches, available at counters in cafés and bars) from €1.10; *cichetti* (hot and cold tapas at wine bars) from €2 per item; full meal for one at an inexpensive restaurant €25–30; at a moderate restaurant, including cover and service (excluding drinks) €40–5; pizza €6–12; beer €3–5; glass of house wine €2–5.

Hotel. For bed and breakfast per night in high season, inclusive of tax: deluxe, €400 and above; expensive, €250–400; moderate, €130–250; inexpensive, less than €130.

Lido Beach. Cabins up to €100/day.

Museums and Attractions. €4–10. A museum pass for all civic museums costs €18.

Porters. One piece of luggage costs €18 and two pieces €24.

Public Transport. Vaporetto: single fare €6.50; 24-hour ticket €16; 72-hour ticket €31.

C

CLIMATE

Venetian winters are cold, summers are hot, and the weather the rest of the year somewhere in between. The winds off the Adriatic and occasional flooding mean that Venice can be damp and chilly, although very atmospheric, between November and March. June, July and August can be stifling – air-conditioning is pretty essential for a good night's rest at this time of year.

CLOTHING

A pair of comfortable walking shoes is essential – despite Venice's excellent canal transport network, if you want to sightsee, you'll probably spend most of your time on foot. For summer, pack thin cotton clothing and a light jacket for breezy evening vaporetto rides. Remember that when visiting churches you won't be allowed in if your back and shoulders are uncovered or if your shorts go above the knee. For winter trips, take lots of layers, including a warm coat. Some of the posher hotels loan out boots in case of light flooding but it's a good idea to bring your own waterproof footwear with you anyway.

Venice is generally an informal city, but stylish dress is expected at its smarter restaurants. Men must wear a jacket and tie to gain entry to the Casino.

CRIME AND SAFETY

Although Venice is one of the safest cities in Italy, pickpockets and purse-snatchers are not uncommon, and tourists are favourite targets, especially in the crowded areas around Rialto and San Marco. Carry with you only what is absolutely necessary; leave passports, airline tickets and all but one credit card in the hotel safe. Use a money belt or carry your valuables in an inside pocket. For women, a small purse with strings, worn strapped across the body or under a coat in winter, is sensible.

Be careful on crowded public transport, especially when getting on and off the vaporetti, in the crush around San Marco and in deserted streets.

Make photocopies of your passport, airline tickets, driving licence and other vital documents to facilitate reporting any theft and obtaining replacements. Notify the police immediately of any theft, so that they can give you a statement to file with your insurance claim.

Women should avoid dark, out-of-the-way places, although any danger is usually in terms of being hassled, not in being attacked.

CUSTOMS AND ENTRY REQUIREMENTS

For citizens of EU countries, a valid passport or identity card is all that is needed to enter Italy for stays of up to 90 days. Citizens of Australia, Canada, New Zealand and the US require only a valid passport.

Visas. For stays of more than 90 days a visa *(permesso di soggiorno)* or residence permit is required. Regulations change from time to time, so check with the Italian Embassy in your home country before you travel.

Customs. Free exchange of non-duty-free goods for personal use is allowed between countries within the European Union (EU). Refer to your home country's regulating organisation for a current list of import restrictions.

Currency Restrictions. Tourists may bring an unlimited amount of Italian or foreign currency into the country.

Above from far left: Hotel Danieli; bridge and colourful houses in Castello.

D

DISABLED TRAVELLERS

Although Venice's narrow alleys and numerous stepped bridges make the city difficult to negotiate for disabled travellers, there are ways and means of getting around and seeing at least some of the major sights. The larger vaporetti (such as nos 1 and 2) have access for wheelchairs, although the slimmer *motoscafi* should be avoided.

If you speak Italian, the Informahandicap organisation has a useful website at www.comune.venezia.it/informahandicap and a branch at Ca'-Farsetti, Riva del Carbon, San Marco 4136; tel: 041-274 8144. The main tourist office in the Venice Pavilion *(see p.105)* supplies maps with useful itineraries marking accessible areas, bridges with ramps for wheelchairs and toilets for the disabled. Keys to operate the accessible bridges are available from the tourist office. The tourist office (APT) *Where to Stay* booklet indicates which hotels are wholly or partially suitable for disabled people.

Accessible attractions (note that no differentiation is made between full and partial access) include the Basilica San Marco, Palazzo Ducale, Ca' Rezzonico, the churches of the Frari, La Salute, San Zanipolo and San Giorgio Maggiore and the Museo Correr.

DRIVING

Venice is a traffic-free zone, and the closest you can get to the centre in a car is Piazzale Roma, where there are two large multi-storey car parks. There is also a huge multi-level car park on the adjacent 'car-park' island of Tronchetto, the terminal for the car ferry to the Lido, where driving is allowed. There are also two car parks on the mainland at Mestre San Giuliano and Fusina, both of which have easy access to Venice by bus.

Although the outdoor car parks are guarded night and day, it's sensible not to leave anything of value in your car.

E

ELECTRICITY

The electrical current is 220V, AC, and sockets take two-pin round-pronged plugs. Bring a multiple adaptor *(una presa multipla)*, as required.

EMBASSIES AND CONSULATES

Most consulates have useful lists of English-speaking doctors, lawyers and interpreters, etc.

Australia (Embassy): Via Antonio Bosio 5, Rome; tel: 06-852 721, www.italy.embassy.gov.au.
Canada (Consulate): Riviera Ruzzante 25, Padua; tel: 049-876 4833.
New Zealand (Embassy): Via Clitunno 44, Rome; tel: 06-853 7501, www.nzembassy.com.
Republic of Ireland (Embassy): Piazza di Campitelli 3, Rome; tel: 06-697 9121, www.embassyofireland.it.
South Africa (Consulate): Santa

Croce 466, Piazzale Roma; tel: 041-524 1599.

UK (Consulate): Piazzale Donatori di Sangue 2, Mestre; tel: 041-505 5990, www.ukve.it.

US (Consulate): via Principe Amedeo 2/10, Milan; tel: 02-290 351, Milan. usconsulate.gov.

EMERGENCIES

In case of an emergency, tel:
Ambulance: 118
Fire: 115
Carabinieri: 112 (urgent police action)
Police: 113

G

GUIDES AND TOURS

The tourist office *(see p.105)* can supply you with a list of qualified tour guides if you want a personal tour of a particular site or on a specialist aspect of Venice. All year round there are standard tours (book through hotels and travel agencies), including a two-hour walking tour of San Marco, taking in the Basilica and the Palazzo Ducale; a two-hour walking and gondola tour covering the Frari and the Grand Canal; a one-hour evening gondola serenade tour; and a three-hour islands tour. It costs more to go on an organised tour than to visit the same places independently.

A cruise along the Brenta Canal to Padua, aboard the 200-seater *Burchiello* (www.burchiello.it) motorboat, makes an interesting (and expensive) day out;

book through local travel agencies/hotels. The return journey is by coach.

Chorus Churches

Chorus (tel: 041-2750462, www.chorus venezia.org; *see also p.13*), a programme that promotes the preservation of the city's churches, offers guided tours from Mar–Jun and Sept–Dec to a number of churches. A discount pass (€9) is also offered by this group – valid for entrance to 15 churches, the pass may be bought at any of the participating churches. Free tours are given of the Basilica in summer, while 'Secret Routes' (*Itinerari Segreti*; charge) show you the ins and outs of life at the Palazzo Ducale.

Evening lectures on the art and history of Venice are held during the summer months. Ask at the tourist office for details. For more information on guided tours consult www.toursitaly.com.

H

HEALTH AND MEDICAL CARE

EU residents should obtain an EHIC (European Health Insurance Card), available from post offices or online at www.ehic.org.uk, which entitles them to emergency medical/hospital *(ospedale)* treatment by reciprocal agreement.

For US citizens: if your private health insurance policy does not cover you while abroad (note that Medicare does not have coverage outside the US), take out a short-term policy before leaving home.

Ask at your hotel if you need a doctor/dentist who speaks English. The US and British consulates *(see p.98–9)* have lists of English-speaking doctors. Many doctors at Venice's main hospital, next to San Zanipolo, speak English; for casualty *(pronto soccorso)*, where medical emergencies are handled, tel: 041-529 4516.

Mosquitoes: These can be a big nuisance in Venice in summer, so take along a small plug-in machine that burns a tablet emitting fumes that are noxious to them. Airport shops sell these, and some hotels also provide them. Take cream with you to soothe bites.

Pharmacies: Italian *farmacias* open during shopping hours and in turn for night and holiday service; the address of the nearest open pharmacy is posted on all pharmacy doors. You can also check the list in *Un Ospite di Venezia (see p.101)* or consult the local press.

L

LANGUAGE

All Venetian hotels above a basic standard will have staff who speak some English, French or German, and unless you go well off the beaten track you should have no problem communicating in shops or restaurants. However, in bars and cafés away from Piazza San Marco, you'll almost certainly have the chance to practise your Italian, and the locals will think more of you for making an effort. Note that

in Italian the letter 'c' is pronounced 'ch' (as in church) when it is followed by 'e' or 'i,' while 'ch' is a hard sound, like the 'c' in cat.

For a list of useful Italian vocabulary, see the back cover of the pull-out map that comes with this book, or the inside of the back-cover flap.

Venetian Dialect

Venetians have a strong dialect, though to the visitor unfamiliar with the Italian language this is academic. However, some terms are useful to know: there is only one *piazza* in Venice – San Marco; other squares are usually called *campo*, although a small square may be known as a *piazzetta*; the term *calle* is used to refer to most streets, but a *salizzada* is a main street, and a covered passage is a *sottoportego*. A *ponte* is a bridge, a canal is a *rio*, and the broad paved walkway along a major waterfront or *canale* is a *riva* or a *fondamenta*.

The following is a list of useful Venetian terms:
Ca' (from casa): house/palace
calle: alley
campo: square
campiello: small square
corte: external courtyard
cortile: internal courtyard
fontego or *fondaco*: historic warehouse
fondamenta: wide quayside
punta: a point
ramo: side street or dead end
rio (plural *rii*): curving canal lined by buildings
rio terrà: in-filled canal
riva: promenade, quayside

ruga: broad shopping street
rughetta: small shopping street
sacca: inlet
salizzada: main street; means 'paved'
sottoportico (or *sottoportego*):
tiny alleyway running under a building
squero: boatyard
stazio: gondoliers' station

Notice that both Venetian and Italian names are used in street signs and on maps: for example, San Giuliano is 'San Zulian' and Santi Giovanni e Paolo is 'San Zanipolo' (Giovanni becomes 'Zani' in dialect).

LOST PROPERTY

The lost property *(oggetti rinvenuti)* office, Ufficio Oggetti Rinvenuti, is located at Ca' Loredan on Riva del Carbon, 4136 San Marco, near the Rialto Bridge (tel: 041-274 8225; Mon–Fri 8.30am–12.30pm and Mon, Thur 2.30pm–4.30pm). If you lose something on a vaporetto, go to the lost property office (daily 9am–8pm) in the ACTV building at Piazzale Roma. There are also lost property offices at the airport (tel: 041-260 6436) and railway station (tel: 041-785 238).

MAPS

For those who plan to stay in Venice any length of time, a worthwhile investment is *Calli, Campielli e Canali*, a volume of very detailed street maps of Venice and its lagoon.

MEDIA

Print Media

Newspapers and magazines *(giornali, riviste)*. You can find both American and British English-language newspapers at airports and in most city-centre news-stands *(edicola)*; some are available on the day of publication, others with a delay of 24 hours. For those who wish to get a little Venetian insight and can read Italian, the local newspaper is *Il Gazzettino*. National paper *La Repubblica* occasionally contains a section in English.

Listings Magazines

Venice's useful free listings magazine *Un Ospite di Venezia* comes out fortnightly in season, monthly off season, but is only available in print form in a few hotels (mostly the grand ones); it is, however, also available online at www.unospitedivenezia.it. It details visitor attractions, events and exhibitions, including opening times and prices, and also has a useful section on practical information.

La Rivista di Venezia (Venice Magazine) features articles on culture and news in English and Italian and includes a *What's On* booklet. The city's tourist offices also issue a free calendar of opening times, shows and events.

Television

The Italian state television network, the RAI (Radio Televisione Italiana), broadcasts three TV channels, which compete with six independent ones. All programmes are in Italian, including British and American feature films and

imports, which are dubbed. Most hotels have cable connections for CNN Europe, CNBC and other channels that offer world news in English including BBC World and Sky.

Radio

The airwaves are crammed with radio stations, most of them broadcasting popular music. The BBC World Service can be picked up on shortwave radio.

MONEY

Currency. Italy's monetary unit is the euro (€), which is divided into 100 cents. Banknotes are available in denominations of 500, 200, 100, 50, 20, 10 and 5 euros. There are coins for 2 and 1 euros, and for 50, 20, 10, 5, 2 and 1 cents.

Currency Exchange. Currency exchange offices *(cambio)* are usually open Monday to Friday, although hours do vary, and some open all day; some also stay open on Saturday. Both *cambio* and banks charge a commission. Banks generally offer higher exchange rates and lower commissions. Passports are usually required when changing money.

ATMs. Automatic currency-exchange machines *(bancomat)* are operated by most banks and provide a convenient way of taking out money. Independent (non-bank related) ATMs can also be found in the centre of town.

Credit Cards and Traveller's Cheques. Most hotels, shops and restaurants take credit cards. If the card's sign is posted in the window of a business, they must accept it, although some may try to avoid doing so. Traveller's cheques are accepted almost everywhere, but you will usually get better value if you exchange them at a bank. Passports are needed when cashing traveller's cheques.

OPENING HOURS

Banks. Hours are Mon–Fri 8.30am–1.30pm, 2.35–3.35pm.

Bars and Restaurants. Some café-bars open for breakfast, but others do not open until around noon; the vast majority shut early, at around 10.30 or 11pm. Nearly all restaurants close at least one day a week; some close for parts of August, January and February.

Churches. The 15 Chorus Churches *(see p.13 and 99)* open Mon–Sat 10am–5pm. The Frari is also open Sun 1–6pm. Other churches are normally open Mon–Sat from around 8am until noon and from 3 or 4pm until 6 or 7pm. Sunday openings vary, some are only open for morning services.

Museums and Galleries. Some close one day a week (usually Mon/Tue), but otherwise open at 9 or 10am until 6pm.

Shops. Business hours are Monday to Saturday, 9 or 10am until 1pm, and 3 or 4pm until 7pm. Some shops are open all day and even on Sundays, particularly in peak season.

P

POLICE

Although you rarely see or need them
Venice's police (*polizia* or *carabinieri*
– the latter for more serious matters)
function efficiently and are courteous.
The emergency police telephone
number is 112 or 113; this will put you
through to a switchboard and someone
who speaks your language.

POST OFFICES

The main office (*ufficio postale*; Mon–
Sat 8.30am–6.30pm) is inside the Fon-
dacho dei Tedeschi at the Rialto. The
two main sub-offices (both Mon– Fri
8.30am–2pm, Sat 8.30am– 1pm) are on
the Zattere (Dorsoduro) and Calle del-
l'Ascensione, off Piazza San Marco. The
lobby of the main office can be used 24
hours a day for faxes and express post.

Postage stamps (*francobolli*) are sold at
post offices and tobacconists (*tabacchi*),
marked by a distinctive 'T' sign.

PUBLIC HOLIDAYS

Banks, government offices and most
shops and museums close on public
holidays (*giorni festivi*). When a major
holiday falls on a Thursday or a
Tuesday, Italians may make a *ponte*
(bridge) to the weekend, meaning that
Friday or Monday is taken, too.

The most important holidays are:

1 January Capodanno/
　　　　　　Primo dell'Anno

6 January Epifania
25 April Festa della Liberazione
1 May Festa del Lavoro
　　　　　　(Labour Day)
15 August Ferragosto (Assumption)
1 November Ognissanti (All Saints)
8 December Immacolata Concezione
　　　　　　(Immaculate Conception)
25 December Natale (Christmas Day)
26 December Santo Stefano
　　　　　　(Boxing Day)
Moveable Date Pasquetta
　　　　　　(Easter Monday)

The Festa della Salute on 21
November and the Redentore on the
third Sunday of July are special Venetian
holidays, when many shops close.

R

RELIGION

Although predominantly Roman
Catholic, Venice has congregations of
all the major religions (*see list below*).
Check *Un Ospite di Venezia (see p.101)*
or ask at your hotel or the local tourist
office for further details.

Anglican. Church of St George,
Campo San Vio, Dorsoduro.

Evangelical Lutheran. Campo Santi
Apostoli, Cannaregio.

Evangelical Waldensian/Methodist.
Santa Maria Formosa, Castello.

Greek Orthodox. Ponte dei Greci,
Castello.

Jewish Synagogue. Campo del
Ghetto Vecchio 1149, Cannaregio (tel:
041-715 012 or enquire at the Jewish
Community Centre, Campo del
Ghetto Nuovo for more details).

Roman Catholic. Basilica San Marco. Masses in Italian; confession in several languages in the summer.

S

SMOKING

In 2005, smoking was banned in public enclosed spaces throughout Italy. Businesses may be fined up to €2,000 euros, while smokers can face a fine up to €275 for breaking this law.

T

TELEPHONES

The country code for Italy is 39, and the area code for the city of Venice is 041. Note that you must dial the '041' prefix even when making local calls within the city of Venice.

Telephone Boxes. Telecom Italia public phones are found across the city. For these you need coins or phone cards *(schede telefoniche)*, which are sold in tobacconists and post offices. There are also pre-paid international phone cards, which offer good value for phoning abroad; for these you need to dial a toll-free number found on the back of the card. Note that you must insert a coin or a card to access a dial tone even when making a toll-free call.

Mobile Phones. EU mobile (cell) phones can be used in Italy, but check compatibility before you leave. It may be worth buying an Italian SIM card, available from any mobile-phone shop, if you intend to stay for more than a few weeks. The major networks available are offered by Telecom Italia (TIM), Vodafone and iWind.

International Calls. To make an international call, dial 00, followed by the country code (Australia +61, Ireland +353, New Zealand +64, South Africa +27, UK +44, US and Canada +1), then the area code (often minus the initial zero) and finally the individual number.

TIME

Italy is one hour ahead of Greenwich Mean Time (GMT). From the last Sunday in March to the last Sunday in October, clocks are put forward an hour.

TIPPING

A service charge of 10 or 12 percent is often added to restaurant bills, so it is not necessary to tip much – perhaps just round the bill up. However, it is normal to tip bellboys, porters, tour guides and elderly gondoliers who help you into and out of your craft at landing stations.

TOILETS

There are public toilets *(toilette, gabinetti)*, usually of a reasonable standard but with a charge, at the airport, railway station, in car parks and some main squares in the city. You can use the facilities in restaurants, bars and cafés but only if you order a drink. *Signori* means men; *signore* means women.

TOURIST INFORMATION

The Italian National Tourist Board (ENIT) has a website at www.enit.it. Offices abroad can provide basic tourist information, including lists of accommodation, in advance of your trip.

Australia Level 4, 46 Market Street, Sydney; tel: 02-9262 1666.

Canada 175 Bloor Street East, Suite 907, South Tower, Toronto, Ontario M4W 3R8; tel: 416-925 3870; www.italiantourism.com.

UK/Ireland 1 Princes Street, London W1B 2AY; tel: 020-7399 3562; www.enit.it.

US

• Chicago: 500 N. Michigan Avenue, Suite 2240, Chicago, IL 60611; tel: 312-644 0996; www.italiantourism.com.

• Los Angeles: 12400 Wilshire Boulevard, Suite 550, Los Angeles CA 90025; tel: 310-820 0098; www.italiantourism.com.

• New York: 630 Fifth Avenue, Suite 1565, New York, NY 10111; tel: 212-245 4822; www.italiantourism.com.

Tourist Information Offices in Venice

The main tourist (APT) office is in the Venice Pavilion beside the Giardinetti Reali (Public Gardens). The office is open daily 10am–6pm. There is a smaller office on the western corner of Piazza San Marco, opposite the entrance to the Museo Correr: San Marco 71/f, Calle dell'Ascensione/Procuratie Nuove, tel: 041-529 8711; daily 9am–3.30pm. Both supply general information and offer booking for tours and events.

The tourist office at the railway station is also useful: APT Venezia, Ferrovia Santa Lucia (daily 8am–6.30pm), as is the one at the airport: APT Marco Polo (daily 9.30am–7.30pm). This mostly deals with accommodation and transport tickets.

To contact the central tourist office for information on events, itineraries, excursions and hotels, etc, e-mail: info@turismovenezia.it or visit www.turismovenezia.it.

Rolling Venice. If you or someone in your party is aged between 14 and 29, enrol with the official youth-orientated discount scheme known as 'Rolling Venice'. For €4, you are entitled to discounts for 25 museums and galleries, 72-hour vaporetto tickets, as well as shopping, restaurant and hotel discounts. You also receive a free guide booklet containing details of interesting walking itineraries. Enrol at the railway station, the ACTV office in Piazzale Roma or any of the tourist (APT) offices.

Venice Card. This innovation, aimed at tourists, comes in two colours: blue, offering unlimited access to local public transport services and toilets, and orange, which also offers access to municipal museums, including the Palazzo Ducale and the main churches. Both cards also entitle you to discounts on some hotels, hostels, restaurants and shops. Cards can be bought for 1, 3 or 7 days. You can book online at www.venicecard.com, 48 hours in advance. You will be issued

with a voucher, which can then be exchanged for the card at one of the VELA offices (Piazzale Roma, Santa Lucia railway station, Tronchetto car park or Marco Polo airport).

Alternatively you can reserve a card by phoning the call centre (tel +39 041 2424 from abroad) and obtaining a code-number, which can then be exchanged for the card at a VELA office. The price structure is quite complex and depends on age and length of stay.

TRANSPORT

Getting to Venice

By Air. Companies flying to Venice from the UK include British Airways (tel: 0870-850 9850, www.ba.com), who operate flights from Gatwick, BMI (tel: 0870-607 0555, www. flybmi. com), who fly from Heathrow, and easyJet (tel: 0905-821 0905, www. easyjet.com), who fly from Gatwick, Bristol and East Midlands airports.

Ryanair (tel: 0906-270 5656; www. ryanair.com) run flights from Stansted to Treviso airport (32km/20 miles from Venice). There are also summer charters on offer to travellers from Gatwick, Manchester, Birmingham and other regional airports. Aer Lingus (tel: 0870-876 5000, www.flyaerlingus.com) operates services from Dublin to Venice.

From the US there are direct seasonal flights to Venice from New York (Delta Airlines, www.delta.com) and from Philadelphia (US Airways, www.usairways.com). Alitalia runs regular flights from New York, Boston, Miami,

Chicago and Los Angeles to Milan and Rome, with onward links to Venice.

From Australia and New Zealand, flights are generally to Rome, with onward connections possible from there.

Within Italy there are direct flights to Venice from Milan, Naples, Rome and Palermo.

By Train. Venice is very well connected by train. Its main station is Stazione Venezia–Santa Lucia (info. tel: 8488-88088). Travel time on the fastest trains is 2 hours 45 minutes to Milan, 3 hours to Florence and 4 hours 30 minutes to Rome.

For international rail tickets and rail passes contact Rail Europe (tel: 0870-584 8848, www.raileurope.co.uk) or Freedom Rail (tel: 0870-757 9898, www.freedomrail.com).

InterRail cards are valid in Italy, as is the Eurailpass for non-European residents (buy yours before you leave home). Contact Rail Europe, 178 Piccadilly, London W1V 0AL (www. raileurope.co.uk).

The Trenitalia Pass (www.trenitalia. com), covering all trains in Italy, is valid for unlimited travel for 4–10 days within a two month period. A Trenitalia Saver Pass for the same period offers a discount for 2–5 people travelling together. Travel on Eurostar Italia, Intercity Plus and other high-speed trains is permitted on payment of a supplement.

By Bus. Buses from within Italy arrive in Venice at Piazzale Roma. There is a particularly good, cheap bus service between Venice and nearby Padua.

By Car. If you travel by car, you will need a current driving licence (with an Italian translation unless it is the standard EU licence) and valid insurance (green card). Additional in- surance cover, including a 'return-home' service, is offered by groups including the British and American Automobile Associations. The Channel Tunnel and Cross-Channel car ferries link the UK with France, Belgium and Holland. Once on the continent, you can put your car on a train to Milan (starting points include Boulogne and Paris), from where you can travel to Venice.

Having a car won't help you once you reach Venice, however, as they are not allowed in the centre and must be left in a car park. The huge multi-storey car park at Piazzale Roma is close to the centre and has good ferry services but is pricey (www.asmvenezia.it). Further away is the island of Tronchetto: the largest car park in Europe (tel: 041-520 7555; www.veniceparking. it).Ferry line 82 links Tronchetto with central Venice.

Airports

Two airports serve Venice: Marco Polo and Treviso.

Venice Marco Polo is Venice's main airport, located 13km (8 miles) north of the city. It has a new terminal and sports all the usual amenities expected of an international airport, including hotel and tourist-information booths, bank and currency-exchange offices *(cambio)*, restaurants, shops and internet access. Assistance for wheelchair travellers is available. For flight information, tel: 041-260 9260 or visit www.veniceairport.it.

Public buses (ACTV) run from the airport to the terminus at Piazzale Roma every half-hour in summer and about once an hour in winter; airport buses (ATVO) have a similar timetable. Both are inexpensive (the ACTV service is the cheaper of the two, but very awkward if you have luggage) and take around 30 minutes to reach Piazzale Roma. Buy your tickets from ATVO office in the arrivals terminal. Once at Piazzale Roma (in Santa Croce, just across the Grand Canal from the train station), board the no. 1 vaporetto (waterbus) for an all-stages ride along the Grand Canal; take the no. 2 if you just want the quickest route to San Marco. The new Ponte Calatrava also connects you by foot to the main railway station.

The Alilaguna water launches provide a year-round direct service between Marco Polo airport and central Venice (www.alilaguna.it). Linea Rossa (Red Line) stops at Murano, Lido, Arsenale, San Marco and Zattere (Dorsoduro). Linea Blu (Blue Line) stops at Murano, Fondamente Nuove, Lido, Riva degli Schiavoni and San Marco.

Private water taxis *(taxi acquei)* are the fastest means to reach the centre (30 mins) but are very expensive, so be careful not to confuse them with the Alilaguna craft *(see above)*. However, they will take you right up to your hotel if it has a water entrance, or drop you off as close as possible.

For all forms of water transport from Marco Polo airport you have to walk

about 500m from the new terminal to the small dock area. The shuttle bus service that used to link the two has been suspended.

Treviso is a small airport 32km (20 miles) north of Venice, used mainly by charter companies and low-cost airlines such as Ryanair, who often, confusingly, call it 'Venice airport'. ATVO's Eurobus runs between Treviso airport and Piazzale Roma, connecting with most flights. Alternatively, the no. 6 bus runs from the airport to Treviso's train station, where regular services take 30 minutes to reach Santa Lucia station in central Venice.

Public Transport

Vaporetti *(*Waterbuses). The only public transport in Venice is waterborne, and an efficient vaporetto will take you to within a short walk of anywhere you want to get to. Venice is so compact, however, that for short journeys, it is often quicker (and a good deal cheaper) to walk.

Vaporetti ply the Grand Canal, go round to the north shore of the city (where the main stop is Fondamente Nuove) and shuttle to and from the minor islands. They run regularly throughout the day and provide a wonderful perspective on the city. A schedule for all vaporetti lines may be obtained from the Centro Informazioni ACTV at Piazzale Roma, tel: 041-2424; www.actv.it.

It's best to buy your ticket in advance from the ticket offices that are on, or close to, the landing stages at the main stops, or at any shop displaying an ACTV sign. At the time of press, the individual fare was €6.50 for any single ticket (this is valid for 90 minutes; more than one trip is allowed). However, you can buy one-, three- and seven-day passes as well as family or group fares. A 24-hour or 72-hour pass is a good investment if you intend seeing much of the city (or if you want to use the vaporetti simply to hop across the Grand Canal). If you haven't bought a ticket before boarding, you can purchase one on board from the conductor for a small surcharge.

Venice has recently switched to using an electronic pass called iMob in place of regular tickets. These must be swiped to in front of the small electronic scanners on each landing to validate them; they are also rechargeable, so once you run out of money on your card, you can have pay to have more journeys placed on it.

The main services are: no. 1 *(accelerato)*, which stops at every landing stage along the Grand Canal; no. 2 *(diretto)*, provides a faster service down the Grand Canal as part of its circular San Marco, Giudecca canal, Piazzale Roma route (and the Lido in season).

Nos 41 (anticlockwise) and 42 (clockwise) describe Venice in a circular route, calling at San Zaccaria, Il Redentore (Palladio's masterpiece), Piazzale Roma, Ferrovia (the railway station), Fondamente Nuove, San Michele, Murano and Sant'Elena. Vaporetti 51 and 52 also provide long, scenic, circular tours around the periphery of Venice, as well as stopping

at Murano; in summer they go on to the Lido (you must change at Fondamente Nuove to do the whole route).

Note that the circular routes no longer serve the Arsenale, travelling instead up the Cannaregio canal, stopping at Guglie, and then skirting the northern shores of Venice, including Fondamente Nuove and the Madonna dell'Orto (Tintoretto's church), the shipyards (Bacini stop), San Pietro di Castello and, eventually, the Lido.

Nos 61 and 62 provide a fast route between Piazzale Roma and the Lido, going via the Zattere (Giudecca canal). For the island of Burano you need to take the LN (Laguna Nord) line which departs from Fondamente Nuove and goes via Murano. Line T connects Burano with Torcello.

Traghetti. The *traghetto* (ferry) service operates at various points across the Grand Canal. It is customary (but not obligatory) to stand while crossing. The cost of using the *traghetto* is €0.50.

Water Taxis. If you need a door-to-door service (or you want to avoid the crowds), ask your hotel to call a *motoscafo*. Although fast, they are, however, extremely expensive.

W

WEBSITES

For on-line sites that will help you to plan your trip, the following are good places to start: www.turismo venezia.it, the website of the local tourist board,

and www.meeting venice.it, the site of the Regional Tourist Board, which offers information on hotels, events, restaurants and museum opening times. The City Council's site, www. comune.venezia.it, gives useful links.

Other sites with information on hotels, events and things to do include www.veneziasi.it, www.initaly.com, www.hellovenezia.com and www. veniceonline.it. For waterbus maps and timetables consult www.actv.it.

Internet Cafés.

Venice has a cluster of internet cafes, including Net House Internet Café (Campo Santo Stefano) and Libreria Mondadori (San Marco).

WOMEN

Venice is an extremely safe city, but, as anywhere in Italy, women may be taken aback by the amount of attention they receive. Most of this attention comes in the form of lingering glances or the calls of '*bella*'; the best approach is to ignore the looks and comments and move on.

YOUTH HOSTELS

There are half a dozen youth hostels (*ostelli della gioventù*) in Venice, with three in Giudecca, the best location. Particularly recommended is Ostello Venezia (Fondamenta delle Zitelle, Giudecca 86; tel: 041-5238211; www. ostellionline.org).

Venice is the most costly city in Italy, and its hotels are notoriously expensive. A simple, central hotel is often the same price as a mid-market hotel elsewhere in Italy. The basic rules when planning your stay are: book early or scan the web for last-minute deals and check which way your room faces and what the price differential is between a tiny room and a palatial room. A hotel may well offer a choice between an expensive large room overlooking the Grand Canal, and a tiny back room overlooking a bleak courtyard. Even so, a room with a view can still cost half as much again as one without a view.

The closer you are to San Marco, the higher the price of accommodation, with the exception of a few expensive hotels on the Lido, Giudecca and San Clemente. Delightful, central and convenient though the San Marco area is, it feels resolutely touristy, so visitors would do well to broaden their horizons. This can mean choosing somewhere in Castello, where the spread of upmarket hotels and newly converted boutique hotels makes it a good choice. Or try an individualistic boutique hotel in the up-and-coming Cannaregio area. Although no longer a bargain, the tranquil, romantic Dorsoduro district is charming, with small but sought-after

mid-market hotels. For families with young children, the Lido makes a good choice, with its sandy beaches and bike rides, but remains the least Venetian area of Venice. The budget alternative is the station area, which is convenient rather than attractive.

If staying outside the city, avoid the rather soulless Mestre and opt for the atmospheric Padua or Treviso, a 30-minute train ride from Venice.

San Marco

Flora

Calle della Pergola, off Calle Larga XXII Marzo; tel: 041-520 5884; fax: 041-522 8217; www.hotelflora.it; vaporetto: Santa Maria del Giglio; €€€
A sought-after, family-run hotel set in a quiet alley near St Mark's. Bedrooms can be palatial or poky (the best are nos 45, 46 and 47, graced with *fin-de-siècle* furnishings). Breakfast in the secluded courtyard garden.

Gritti Palace

Campo Santa Maria del Giglio; tel: 041-794 611; fax: 041-520 0942; www.starwoodhotels.com; vaporetto: Santa Maria del Giglio; €€€€
Hemingway, Churchill and Greta Garbo all stayed in this 15th-century palace. The most patrician hotel in Venice, it retains the air of a private *palazzo*, with Murano chandeliers and damask furnishings.

La Fenice et des Artistes

Campiello della Fenice; tel: 041-523 2333; fax: 041-520 3721; www. fenicehotels.it; vaporetto: San Marco-

---

Price for a double room for one night without breakfast:

€€€€	over 500 euros
€€€	280–500 euros
€€	150–280 euros
€	below 150 euros

Vallaresso or Santa Maria del Giglio; €€

Within a stone's throw of the Fenice opera house, this hotel is popular with singers and musicians. There's a new and an old section, both of which are furnished in traditional style.

Locanda Art Deco

Calle delle Botteghe; tel: 041-277 0558; fax: 041-270 2891; www. locandaartdeco.com; vaporetto: Sant'Angelo or Accademia; €€

Locanda Art Deco (with an interior in that style) is a quiet, good-value hotel in a 17th-century *palazzo*. Good location just off Campo Santo Stefano.

Locanda Novecento

Calle del Dose; tel: 041-241 3765; fax: 041-520 3721; www.locanda novecento.it; vaporetto: Santa Maria del Giglio; €€

An exotic touch of Marrakesh in Venice, with funky Moroccan lamps and Turkish rugs. There are beamed ceilings, cosy bedrooms and a tiny courtyard for breakfast.

Luna Baglioni

Calle Vallaresso/Calle Larga dell' Ascensione; tel: 041-528 9840; fax: 041-528 7160; www.baglionihotels. com; vaporetto: San Marco-Vallaresso; €€€€

The oldest hotel in Venice, this was originally a Knights Templar lodge for pilgrims en route to Jerusalem. Just off Piazza San Marco, it has Venetian décor, an 18th-century ballroom and the grandest breakfast room in Venice.

Monaco e Grand

Calle Vallaresso; tel: 041-520 0211; fax: 041-520 0501; www.hotel monaco.it; vaporetto: San Marco-Vallaresso; €€€€

A mix of slick contemporary and classic Venetian style. Chic bar and waterfront breakfast room. The hotel's newer Palazzo Salvadego annexe is more typically Venetian.

Santo Stefano

Campo Santo Stefano; tel: 041-520 0166; fax: 041-522 4460; www.hotel santostefanovenezia.com; vaporetto: Sant'Angelo or Accademia; €€€

Set in a 15th-century watchtower overlooking one of the city's most stylish squares, this hotel gives a friendly, unjaded impression. There are spa baths throughout, and breakfast is served on the square.

Saturnia & International

Calle Larga XXII Marzo; tel: 041-520 8377; fax: 041-520 5858; www. hotelsaturnia.it; vaporetto: Santa Maria del Giglio; €€€

The mood of this distinctive hotel is vaguely medieval in inspiration, which may seem either romantic or austere. Bedrooms are intimate and comfy.

Castello

Casa Querini

Campo San Giovanni Novo; tel: 041-241 1294; fax: 041-2414231; www.locandaquerini.com; vaporetto: San Zaccaria or Rialto; €€

A small inn close to Campo Santa Maria Formosa. It has 11 spacious,

Above from far left: bedroom at the Gritti Palace; Junior Suite at the Luna Baglioni.

low-key rooms, decorated in 17th-century Venetian style and pleasant staff.

Colombina

Calle del Remedio; tel: 041-277 0525; fax: 041-277 6044; www. hotelcolombina.com; vaporetto: San Zaccaria; €€€

Boutique hotel close to St Mark's with a muted, modern take on Venetian style, slick marble bathrooms and balconies with views of the Bridge of Sighs. The rooms in the cheaper annexe are also in traditional style.

Danieli

Riva degli Schiavoni; tel: 041-522 6480; fax: 041-520 0208; www. starwoodhotels.com/danieli; vaporetto: San Zaccaria; €€€€

Set on the waterfront, this world-famous hotel has a splendid Gothic foyer, and plush rooms with parquet floors and gilded bedsteads; splendid rooftop restaurant.

Liassidi Palace

Ponte dei Greci; tel: 041-520 5658; fax: 041-522 1820; www.liassidi palacehotel.com; vaporetto: San Zaccaria; €€€

A boutique hotel in a Gothic palace behind the Riva degli Schiavoni with a muted yet sleek interior. The individualistic bedrooms range from Art Deco to Bauhaus. Bar but no restaurant.

Locanda La Corte

Calle Bressana; tel: 041-241 1300; fax: 041-241 5982; www.locanda lacorte.it; vaporetto: Ospedale; €

Small Gothic palace off Campo SS Giovanni e Paolo. The décor is a muted version of the traditional Venetian style. There's an inner courtyard for breakfast. Bedrooms overlook the canal or the courtyard.

Locanda Vivaldi

Riva degli Schiavoni; tel: 041-277 0477; fax: 041-277 0489; www. locandavivaldi.it; vaporetto: San Zaccaria; €€€

On the lagoon and partially set in the house where Vivaldi once lived (his music is often piped into the public rooms). Bedrooms are romantic and individualistic; many have jacuzzis. Breakfast is taken on the roof terrace.

Londra Palace

Riva degli Schiavoni; tel: 041-520 0533; fax: 041-522 5032; www.hotelondra.it; vaporetto: San Zaccaria; €€€€

This elegant hotel, where the Russian composer Tchaikovsky wrote his Fourth Symphony in 1877, has been restored to its old splendour. It's comfortable and civilised with a gourmet restaurant, a lovely terrace and very welcoming staff.

Metropole

Riva degli Schiavoni; tel: 041-520 5044; fax: 041-522 3679; www.hotel metropole.com; vaporetto: San Zaccaria; €€€€

This family-owned boutique hotel has been renovated and is now dotted with eclectic antiques and objets d'art. It has a Michelin-starred restaurant, trendy bar, lovely garden courtyard and lagoon

or canal views; rooms can be cosy (try no. 350) or amusingly kitsch (no. 251).

Palazzo Schiavoni

Fondamenta dei Furlani; tel: 041-241 1275; fax: 041-241 4490; www. palazzoschiavoni.com; vaporetto: San Zaccaria; €€

Rooms and apartments in a tasteful conversion (with the odd frescoed ceiling) beside the Scuola di San Giorgio. A good choice for families.

Dorsoduro

Accademia Villa Marevege

Fondamenta Bollani; tel: 041-521 0188; fax: 041-523 9152; www. pensioneaccademia.it; vaporetto: Accademia; €€

Gracious, highly sought-after wisteria-clad villa at the Grand Canal end of Rio San Trovaso. Atmospheric bedrooms and lovely canalside gardens.

Ca' Maria Adele

Rio Terrà Catecumeni; tel: 041-520 3078; fax: 041-528 9013; www. camariaadele.hotelinvenice.com; vaporetto: Salute; €€€

This wonderful small boutique hotel is set right next to the Salute, which makes for marvellous views. The hotel has an eclectic mix of Eastern-influenced Venetian décor. For a real splurge, try one of the five themed rooms, such as the Doge's Room, a riot of rich red brocade. Attentive staff.

Ca' Pisani

Rio Terrà Foscarini; tel: 041-240 1411; fax: 041-277 1061;

www.capisanihotel.it; vaporetto: Accademia or Zattere; €€€

In a historic *palazzo* near the Accademia, this is a stylish, Art Deco-style hotel. There's a trendy wine bar/restaurant, and all rooms have satellite television and (novel for Venice) WiFi.

Ca' San Trovaso

Fondamenta delle Eremite; tel: 041-277 1146; fax: 041-277 7190; www.casantrovaso.com; vaporetto: Ca' Rezzonico or San Basilio; €

This unpretentious little hotel on a quiet canal has terracotta floors and damask wallpaper, but no television sor telephones in the rooms. Ask for room 2 or 4. Nice roof terrace.

Locanda San Barnaba

Calle del Traghetto; tel: 041-241 1233; fax: 041-241 3812; vaporetto: Ca' Rezzonico; €€

Small inn near Ca' Rezzonico in a 16th-century frescoed palace run by the ancestral owner. The traditional Venetian-style rooms are pleasant (ask for a frescoed one). Pretty canalside courtyard for breakfast.

Pensione Calcina

Fondamenta Zattere ai Gesuati; tel: 041-520 6466; fax: 041-522 7045; www.lacalcina.com; vaporetto: Zattere; €€

Overlooking the Giudecca canal, this is a romantic inn, where art critic John Ruskin lodged in 1876. Charming roof terrace, uncluttered bedrooms (try no. 127) plus the waterside La Piscina dining room and terrace. Book early.

Above from far left: terrace with unbeatable views at the Luna Baglioni *(see p.111)*; smart stripes at the Londra Palace; foyer at the Locanda Vivaldi.

3749 Ponte Chiodo

Ponte Chiodo; tel: 041-241 3935; fax: 041-241 9583; www.ponte chiodo.it; vaporetto: Ca' d'Oro; €

Located in a quiet area of Cannaregio, this is a budget guesthouse with rare amenities such as WiFi and air conditioning. The friendly owner is known to eat breakfast with his guests and provide valuable information about the city. Breakfast is served in the courtyard in nice weather.

Abbazia

Calle Priuli dei Cavaletti; tel: 041-717 333; fax: 041-717 949; www.abbaziahotel.com; vaporetto: Ferrovia; €€

This former Carmelite foundation has been sensitively restored and has beamed ceilings in tasteful bedrooms plus a courtyard and garden. It's close to the station but tranquil nonetheless.

Ai Mori d'Oriente

Fondamenta della Sensa; tel: 041-711 001; fax: 041-714 209; www.morihotel.com; vaporetto: Madonna dell'Orto; €€€

Quirky boutique hotel with lots of character and eclectic and exotic touches, plus welcoming staff.

Ca' Sagredo

Campo Santa Sofia; tel: 041-241 3111; fax: 041-241 3521; www.casagredohotel.com; vaporetto: Ca' d'Oro; €€€€

One of the newest luxury hotels in Venice, Ca' Sagredo is located in a historic *palazzo* with fabulous frescoes by Tiepolo and Sebastiano Ricci. Many rooms have Grand Canal views, and you can enjoy cocktails on the Canal at the hotel bar. The hotel can also provide a babysitter, personal shopper or personal trainer on request.

Casa del Melograno

Campiello del Ponte Storto; tel: 041-520 8807; fax: 041-275 7703; www.locandadelmelograno.it; vaporetto: San Marcuola; €

Tucked off the busy Strada Nova, this guesthouse is a great budget option. All the rooms have been recently remodelled in a simple modern style. The private garden is open to guests.

Giorgione

Santi Apostoli; tel: 041-522 5810; fax: 041-523 9092; www.hotelgiorgione. com; vaporetto: Ca' d'Oro; €€

Not far from the Ca' d'Oro, this family-run hotel dates to the 14th century. Décor is traditional Venetian, with chandeliers and Murano glass. The breakfast room opens onto a courtyard. Other highlights include free afternoon coffee and cakes.

Grand Hotel Dei Dogi

Fondamenta Madonna dell'Orto; tel: 041-220 8111; fax: 041-722 278; www.deidogi.boscolohotels.com; €€€€; vaporetto: Madonna dell'Orto

Luxury hotel set on the edge of the lagoon. A former monastery, it is still an oasis of calm, with quiet, tasteful

décor and the largest and loveliest hotel garden in Venice.

Oltre Il Giardino

Fondamenta Contarini; tel: 041-275 0015; fax: 041-795 452; www.oltre ilgiardino-venezia.com; vaporetto: San Tomà; €€

Situated near the church of the Frari, this small guesthouse is the former home of Alma Mahler (wife of the composer). Each of the six rooms has been recently renovated in a homely, modern style, and there's also a lovely courtyard where you can enjoy breakfast in nice weather.

The Giudecca

Cipriani

Isola della Giudecca 10; tel: 041-520 7744; fax: 041-520 3930; www. hotelcipriani.com; vaporetto: Zitelle; €€€€

The Cipriani is the most glamorous of Venetian hotels. Lavish bedrooms are furnished with Fortuny fabrics, and there's a pool, gardens, tennis courts, a yacht harbour, and a water-launch that whisks guests to San Marco.

Hilton Molino Stucky

Isola della Guidecca 753; tel: 041-522 1267; fax: 041-522 1267; www. molinostucky hilton.com; vaporetto: Palanca; €€€€

The huge 19th-century flour mill on the Giudecca waterfront has been converted into a 5-star hotel with 380 rooms and Venice's largest congress centre. Facilities include five restaurants, bars, rooftop pool and large spa. The excel-lent service includes a 'magic' button on your telephone that will summon help for almost anything. *See also p.64.*

The Lido and Other Islands

Hôtel des Bains

Lungomare Marconi, Il Lido; tel: 041-526 5921; fax: 041-526 0113; www. starwoodhotels.com/italy; €€€

Atmospheric Belle Epoque hotel that featured in Thomas Mann's *Death in Venice*. Has a private beach on the Lido. Popular with the stars during the Film Festival. *See also p.86–7.*

Locanda Cipriani

Isola di Torcello; tel: 041-730 150; fax: 041-735 433; www.locanda cipriani.com; €€

Small, rustic inn in a seemingly remote spot with excellent homely restaurant; run by a branch of the Cipriani family. Garden for outdoor dining.

Quattro Fontane

Via Quattro Fontane, Il Lido; tel: 041-526 0227; fax: 041-526 0726; www.quattrofontane.com; €€

A quirky, much-loved mock-Tyrolean hotel. The hotel's compound, just a few blocks from the beach, includes tennis courts. Open Apr–Nov only. No lift.

San Clemente Palace

Isola di San Clemente; tel: 041-244 5001; fax: 041-244 5800; www. sanclemente.thi.it; €€€

Luxurious romantic hideaway in a con-verted monastery with a private shuttle from St Mark's. Three restaurants, bars, pool, spa and lovely grounds.

Above from far left: courtyard at the Giorgione; room service – bellinis and pastries – at the Cipriani.

Venetian restaurants range in style from cool, 18th-century elegance – especially in San Marco and Castello – to rustic gentility. Yet individualistic inns abound, tucked under pergolas or spilling onto terraces and courtyards. More upmarket places are termed *ristoranti*, but may be called *osterie* (inns) if they focus on homely food in an intimate or rustic setting. *Bacari* are traditional wine bars that also serve food, a Venetian version of tapas, known as *cichetti*.

San Marco

Acqua Pazza

Campo Sant'Angelo, San Marco 3808; tel: 041-277 0688; closed Mon; vaporetto: S. Angelo; €€€
This lively pizzeria serves authentic Neapolitan pizzas and seafood. Bruschetta, antipasti and a post-coffee limoncello are on the house. All the bread and pasta are made on-site, ensuring quality and freshness.

Al Graspo De Ua

Calle dei Bombaseri; tel: 041-520 0150; closed Sun; vaporetto: Rialto; €€–€€€
Tucked away in the warren of streets en route to the Rialto, this well-established fish restaurant has been serving

Price guide for a two-course meal for one with a glass of house wine:

€€€€	over 60 euros
€€€	40–60 euros
€€	25–40 euros
€	below 25 euros

spider crab, scallops and tagliolini with lobster since 1855.

Antico Martini

Campo San Fantin; tel: 041-522 4121; vaporetto: S. Maria del Giglio; €€€
This classic restaurant, with piano bar and late opening hours, is a Venetian institution. The menu includes seafood risotto, *granseola* (spider crab) and *fegato alla veneziana* (liver on a bed of onions). Booking essential.

Cavatappi

Campo della Guerra, near San Zulian, San Marco 525; tel: 041-296 0252; closed Sun D and Mon; vaporetto: San Zaccaria or Rialto; €€€
A fashionable, contemporary-style wine bar serving good snacks, light lunches and evening meals. The Italian wines and cheeses rotate every few months.

Centrale

Piscina Frezzeria, San Marco 1659b; tel: 041-296 0664; daily 7pm–2am; vaporetto: San Marco Vallaresso; €€€
This futuristic, sleek bar-restaurant and music club feels more Milanese than Venetian. Set in a converted cinema, the 16th-century *palazzo* incorporates cutting-edge design, with high prices to match. Sample a full Mediterranean menu or just snack while chilling out to contemporary sounds. One of the few kitchens open very late at night.

Harry's Bar

Calle Vallaresso, San Marco 1323; tel: 041-528 5777; vaporetto: San Marco Vallaresso; €€€

The fresh, consistent menu of this legendary bar attracts wealthy Venetians as well as visitors. The tone is perfect, set by the current Arrigo (Harry) Cipriani. The legendary bar and restaurant is a place you must visit at least once, and try a Bellini cocktail (the house speciality combining prosecco and peach juice), even if the price puts you off having a second. Despite its fame, it is surprisingly unpretentious.

Trattoria Do Forni

Calle dei Specchieri; tel: 041-523 2148; vaporetto: San Marco Giardinetti; €€€

An upmarket spot masquerading as a trattoria. Reliable cuisine and rambling yet intimate rooms. The menu embraces caviar, oysters, steak and pasta, seafood risotto and Venetian vegetable pie.

Castello

Alle Testiere

Calle del Mondo Novo, Castello 5801; tel: 041-522 7220; closed Sun and Mon; vaporetto: Rialto or San Zaccaria; €€€

Located near Campo Santa Maria Formosa, this small, well-loved restaurant demands booking in advance. Yet another place known for its fresh, great-quality seafood, it also features a fantastic wine list and cheeses from across Italy, many of which are not normally found in Venice.

La Corte Sconta

Calle del Pestrin; tel: 041-522 7024; closed Sun and Mon; vaporetto: Arsenale; €€€

This is a renowned yet authentic venue, tucked into a secret courtyard, with a cheerful atmosphere and a menu based on fish fresh from Chioggia market. You can tuck into fishy antipasti, from scallops and calamari to sea snails, shrimps and sardines. Booking is advisable.

Enoteca Mascareta

Calle Lunga Santa Maria Formosa; tel: 041-523 0744; open D only (7pm–2am); vaporetto: Rialto; €€

A cosy, rustic wine bar, run by wine writer Mauro Lorenzon. You can have salami, ham at the counter, or opt for the menu, including bean soup, lasagne and fish at the table. The convivial host, laid-back jazz and the superb wines ensure a contented clientele.

Hostaria da Franz

Fondamenta San Giuseppe (San Isepe); tel: 041-522 0861; closed Tue; vaporetto: Giardini; €€€

This quaint canalside trattoria was opened in 1842 by an Austrian soldier who fell in love with a Venetian girl. Sample Venetian seafood dishes with a twist, from risotto to gnocchi with prawns and spinach, marinated prawns, grilled fish, or fish with polenta. It's off the beaten track, but convenient for the Biennale gardens. Booking is advisable.

Il Covo

Campiello della Pescaria; tel 041-522 3812; closed Wed and Thur; vaporetto: Arsenale; €€€

With one of the best reputations in the city, foodies from all over pour into this small, elegant restaurant. The fish-heavy

Above from far left: intimately lit *bacaro*; tasty sweets include almond pastries.

Opening Times
Where no closing times are given in the selection below, restaurants are open daily for lunch and dinner.

Reservations
Booking well in advance for fancier restaurants is a must. In addition, due to the fact that locals (especially at weekends) flock to the high-quality, but reasonably priced, eateries, reservations are advisable in general, especially if you would particularly like to dine somewhere. Normally a call the day before or morning of the meal will do the trick, but to avoid disappointment at weekends, book a few days ahead.

menu is excellent. Try the *moeche* (soft-shell crab) lightly fried with onions, or turbot and mussels in a light tomato sauce. It also offers a six-course tasting menu. Booking essential. Smart dress for dinner.

Osteria di Santa Marina

Campo Santa Marina; tel: 041-528 5239; closed all Sun and Mon L; vaporetto: Rialto; €€€

Set in a quiet square, this welcoming restaurant presents reinterpretations of dishes from the Veneto, from cuttlefish ink ravioli with sea bass to seafood pasta, to fresh turbot, tuna, and beef carpaccio, to tuna-and-bean soup and mixed grills; in summer, sit outside on the square and end the experience with a sorbet or cinnamon apple pie.

Trattoria Giorgione

Via Garibaldi; tel 041-522 8727; closed Wed; vaporetto: Giardini; €€

Set in the Arsenale area, this inn is popular with Venetians, both for the traditional fish recipes and for the live folk music most evenings.

Cannaregio

Al Fontego dei Pescaori

Calle Priuli; tel: 041-520 0538; closed Mon; vaporetto: Ca' d'Oro; €€

Lolo, the owner, is president of the Rialto fish market and has his own stall, so the fish is always wonderfully fresh. The wide selection of seafood includes an elegantly presented platter of raw fish, grilled cuttlefish served with white polenta, scallops, sea bass and deep-fried mixed fish.

Al Vecio Bragozzo

Strada Nova, Cannaregio 4386; tel: 041-523 7277; closed Mon; vaporetto: Ca' d'Oro; €€

It can be hard to distinguish between the tourist fare that lies along the Strada Nova, but this restaurant caters to both locals and tourists. The owner's brother owns a fishing *bragozzo* (hence the name), which hauls in fresh seafood each day. Try the delicious and classically Venetian *sardèle in soar* (sardines in an onion sauce with pine-nuts and raisins).

Anice Stellato

Fondamenta della Sensa; tel: 041-720 744; closed Mon–Tue; vaporetto: Guglie or Sant'Alvise; €€

This small, family-run restaurant is a long way from the centre but always busy with locals (book if you can). Come just for the *cichetti* or for a full meal. Far Eastern spices are used widely, making for a quirky twist on Venetian cuisine.

Boccadoro

Campo Widmann, Cannaregio 5405; tel: 041-521 1021; closed Mon; vaporetto: Ca d'Oro; €€€

This local eatery with a fish-based menu is tucked away on a quiet square. The seasonal menu is based on whatever is fresh at the Rialto. The menu is a bit pricey, but includes delicious offerings such as tuna tartare and marinated sea bass. Seating spills out onto the square.

Fiaschetteria Toscana

Salizzada San Giovanni Cristostomo; tel: 041-528 5281; closed all Tue and Wed L; vaporetto: Rialto; €€€

Set near the Rialto Bridge, this is a favourite among local gourmets for excellent, good-value fish and seafood. There is also a smattering of Tuscan steak dishes and cheeses, accompanied by fine wines. Booking recommended.

Vini da Gigio

Fondamenta di San Felice; tel: 041-528 5140; closed Mon and Tue; vaporetto: Ca' d'Oro; €€

A very popular family-run *bacaro* that is both a wine bar and inn, with exceptional food but leisurely service. There's lots of variety, from Venetian risotto to northern Italian game dishes, as well as fine wines. Booking advisable.

San Polo

Ae Do Spade

Calle delle Do Spade, Rialto; tel: 041-521 0583; closed Sun; vaporetto: Rialto Mercato; €€

This place initially looks very touristy, but it is in fact popular with the Venetians. The signature dish is the spicy sandwich known as *paperini*. You can stand at the bar, enjoying their selection of *cichetti* or sit for a full meal from the Venetian menu. The service is prompt and friendly.

Al Nono Risorto

Sottoportego della Siora Bettina, Campo San Cassiano; tel: 041-524 1169; closed Wed; vaporetto: San Silvestro; €€

A rustic spot, framed by a wisteria-hung courtyard and garden. A combination of pizzeria and trattoria, it offers a changing menu of fish, pasta and pizzas.

Particularly popular with thirtysomething Venetians.

Da Fiore

Calle del Scaleter, off Campo di San Polo; tel: 041-721 308; closed Sun and Mon; vaporetto: S. Tomà; €€€€

Possibly the best restaurant in town, and a celebrity haunt during the Film Festival. Local people claim that Da Fiore is an accurate reflection of the subtlety of Venetian cuisine, from grilled calamari and *granseola* (spider crab) to Adriatic tuna, squid, sashimi and *risotto al nero di seppia* (cuttlefish risotto). Only one (much sought-after) table overlooks the canal.

Ruga Rialto

Calle del Sturion, off Ruga Rialto; tel: 041-5211 243; daily 11am–3pm, 6pm–midnight; vaporetto: Rialto Mercato; €€

A bohemian *bacaro* and inn with wooden benches, copper pots and simple but reliable dishes. The menu is small and traditional, at decent prices. Live music often on Friday evenings.

Santa Croce

Al Vecio Fritolin

Calle della Regina; tel: 041-522 2881; closed Mon; vaporetto: San Stae; €€

A *fritolin* is actually a stall or kiosk that serves takeaway fried fish, but here you can enjoy it at the bar or table with a drink. The full menu features mixed fried fish, soft-shell crab and swordfish tartare. A well-known favourite of tourists and locals. Booking is advised.

Above from far left: mozzarella and tomato salad; fresh pasta and fresh pesto, with a sprinkling of pine-nuts and parmesan – the simpler the better; not all Venetian restaurants are in the traditional style.

Meal Times
Most restaurants close between lunch and dinner sittings. Lunch is normally served between 12.30pm and 2.30pm, with dinner service starting around 7pm. Try to adjust to the local time in order to take the best advantage of the menu (go too late, and they may run out of things!). Late-night dining can be difficult to find in Venice, so you'll generally need to settle on somewhere by 9pm.

Alla Zucca

Ponte del Megio; tel: 041-524 1570; closed Sun and all Aug; vaporetto: San Stae; €€

This is an extremely popular trattoria, set by a crooked bridge over the canal, with a few tables outside when the weather is warm. The bohemian atmosphere reflects the eclectic menu, which favours vegetables as well as fish, with creamy pumpkin *(zucca)* flan aubergine pasta and smoked mackerel. Book.

Antica Bessetta

Salizzada de Ca' Zusto; tel: 041-721 687; closed all Tue and Wed L; vaporetto: R.D. Biasio; €€

Off the beaten track, just north of San Giacomo dell'Orio, this is a rustic-style trattoria, but standards are high. It is a temple of Venetian home cooking and a foodies' paradise, with *risi e bisi* (rice and peas), gnocchi, seafood risotto, or the catch of the day, grilled or baked, accompanied by notable regional wines.

Dorsoduro

Ai Gondolieri

Ponte del Formager; tel: 041-528 6396; closed Tue; vaporetto: Salute; €€€

Set close to the Guggenheim, this stylish modern restaurant eschews fish and thrives on a meaty menu, supported by exceptional risotto and good vegetable dishes; try the stuffed baked courgettes (zucchini). Best to book.

Cantinone già Schiavi

Fondamenta Nani, Rio di San Trovaso; tel: 041-523 0034; closes 9.30pm and Sun D; vaporetto: Zattere; €

This old-fashioned canalside wine bar is popular with local people and expats from all walks of life. It's a good place for *cichetti* and snacks – hams, salami and cheese. Savour the mood by popping in for a light lunch at the bar or lingering at the cocktail hour (7–8pm).

La Furatola

Calle Lunga San Barnaba; tel: 041-520 8294; closed Thur; vaporetto: Ca' Rezzonico; €€

A cosy place renowned for its fresh fish, ample portions of pasta (often big enough to share, a practice that is not frowned on) and wonderful desserts. The restaurant takes its name from the small, simple stores that used to provide food for sailors.

Quatro Feri

Calle Lunga San Barnaba; tel: 041-520 6978; closed Sun; vaporetto: Ca' Rezzonico; €€

This bustling new-wave *bacaro* has a youthful owner, Barbara, and her reasonable prices attract a faithful young crowd. Venetian dishes and, as befits a former sommelier, superior wines.

The Giudecca and San Giorgio Maggiore

Altanella

Calle delle Erbe; tel: 041-522 7780; closed Mon and Tue; no credit cards; vaporetto: Palanca or Redentore; €€€

Friendly trattoria favoured by Elton John, who has a home around the corner. Only fish dishes on offer. Lovely outdoor seating with sweeping views across the Giudecca Canal.

Do Mori

Fondamenta Sant'Eufemia; tel: 041-522 5452; closed Sun; vaporetto: San Eufemia; €€

Formed by a breakaway group from Harry's Bar, this is the place for those who can't afford the elevated prices of the original. The food is sound Venetian home cooking, with a preponderance of fish dishes (good scampi risotto) as well as pasta and pizzas.

Fortuny Restaurant

Hotel Cipriani, Fondamenta San Giovanni; tel: 041-520 7744; closed Nov–Mar; vaporetto: Zitelle; €€€

Set in the city's most luxurious hotel, the Fortuny spills onto a glorious terrace. The setting is exquisite, the service divine and the prices deadly. Or try the more informal Cip's Club (prices are lower, but still high). Both offer rare views across to San Marco and free launch service from St Mark's pier. Book ahead.

Harry's Dolci

Fondamenta San Biagio; tel: 041-522 4844; closed Tue and Nov–Feb; vaporetto: S. Eufemia; €€€

Come here for a waterside American brunch; it's Harry's without the hype, and with better views and prices. Try the Venetian risotto, curried chicken or *baccalà mantecato* (salt cod) and sip a signature Bellini in the bar. Tasty pastries served outside mealtimes.

Mistrà

Consorzio Cantieristica Minore (enter on Fondamenta S. Giacomo); tel: 041-522 0743; closed Mon D and Tue; vaporetto: Palanca or Redentore; €€

Make your way through a boatyard to this restaurant, which gives you lovely broad views of the southern lagoon. The menu is a mix of Venetian and Ligurian favourites, owing to the heritage of the owners. At lunch there is a fixed-price menu for workers from the boatyard.

Murano and the Lido

Ai Frati

Fondamenta Venier, Murano; tel: 041-736 694; closed Thur; vaporetto: Murano; €€–€€€

This is Murano's best fish restaurant. If you have the choice, try to get one of the tables on a mooring platform on the canal. The location and neighbourhood bistro atmosphere make it very popular, so be sure to book.

La Taverna

Hotel Westin Excelsior, Lungomare Marconi 41; tel: 041-526 0201; vaporetto: Lido; €€€

This restaurant spreads out under an attractive terrace overlooking the beach. There is a very good buffet with a range of delicious grilled fish. Book.

Trento

Via Sandro Gallo; tel: 041-526 5960; Mon–Sat 7am–9pm, 11pm in summer; vaporetto: Lido; €€

Locals flock to this excellent-value bar/*osteria* at lunchtime for Venetian specialities such as baby octopus, *cotechino* (pork sausage) and salted dried cod.

Above from far left: simple set up at Quatro Feri, an excellent neighbourhood *bacaro*; busy wine bar.

Take Away
Those used to getting having their meal wrapped up to 'take away' at the end of the meal may be met with blank stares in Venice. As Italian portions are quite modest, and freshness is essential to good Italian cuisine, this is not a practice that happens in Italian restaurants.

The traditional take on the city is that entertainment tends to be low-key, focused on piano bars, the historic cafés around San Marco and chic hotel bars. Given that the average age of Venetians is 45, most people opt for cosy drinks in a bar, followed by a meal out, particularly in one of the city's local *bacari*.

While the core clientele of middle-aged Venetians is not about to be shaken from its slumbers by hard-core clubbing, the local nightlife scene is being pushed forward by the large university population at Ca' Foscari or the architecture school IUAV.

Where to Go

If you want romance and glamour, hit the waterfront-hotel piano bars. If elegant designer bars, jazz or lounge-music clubs appeal, most are within walking distance of St Mark's. For traditional *bacari*, set off to Cannaregio or, if it's still early evening, catch the tiny authentic wine bars around the Rialto market; for funkier, reinvented *bacari* Venetian bars, slip off instead to the quieter *campi* and *calli* in areas such as Castello, San Polo or Dorsoduro.

In summer, the nightlife scene switches to the Lido and its seafront grand hotels. As for winter fun, during carnival Venetian nightlife comes into its own, with open-air balls, people-watching and strolling from café to café *(see p.20)*.

San Marco

Centrale (Piscina Frezzeria, off Frezzeria; www.centrale-lounge.com; Mon–Sat 7pm–2am) is an inviting haunt for metropolitan night owls of all ages. Set in a converted cinema in an ancient *palazzo*, this stylish lounge bar is moody and modern, a great place for chilling out with cocktails or dinner. In terms of class and style, its only rivals are the top hotel bars and Harry's, though, on a good night, **Bacaro Lounge** (on Salizzada San Moise), owned by the Benetton family, is also very stylish. **Bacaretto** (Calle delle Botteghe; closed Sat, Sun) is a bar and inn popular with ordinary Venetians. **Torino@notte** (Campo San Luca; www.musicaincampo.com) is a youthful late-night drinking den. **Aurora Café** (Piazza San Marco 50; www.aurora.st; 8pm–2am) switches management in the evening, turning into a cool lounge with DJ sets and injecting the historic square with a bit of modernity.

Castello

Most upmarket nightlife revolves around the large international hotels on the Riva degli Schiavoni, including **Londra Palace** *(see p.112)* with its piano bar, dinner jazz and waterside terrace, and the Danieli, with its great bar and terrace. By contrast, the Metropole hotel *(see p.112)* houses an exotic oriental-style **Zodiac Bar** and holds DJ-led lounge and classic chill evenings every Thursday, accompanied by food- and wine-tastings.

A new entry on the scene, the cosy, modern **Club947** supperclub (club947@hotmail.it or tel: 347-427 9658 to reserve) is making its mark in Campo Santi Filippo e Giacomo.

Dorsoduro

Campo Santa Margherita is the centre of Venice's nightlife, and is awash with buzzing, youth-oriented bars. The red-tinged Bar Rosso *(see p.60)* competes with the futuristic Orange lounge bar (with garden) and the friendly but fake Green Pub, leaving the more low-key Margaret Duchamp bar to cater to a sophisticated crowd. Imagina (Rio Terra canal) is an arty, designer bar that comes into its own at night, with eclectic music and late-night snacks. Cocktails tend to draw a bohemian crowd of painters and writers, while it becomes more relentlessly youth-orientated as the night wears on. La Rivista, connected to the Ca' Pisani Hotel *(see p.113)*, often holds wine-tastings and draws a young, mostly Venetian crowd. **Senso Unico** (Calle della Chiesa, close to the Guggenheim) styles itself as an English pub but does an equally good line in wine and bar snacks. **Suzie Café** (Campo San Basilio) stages live music in summer, from rock to reggae and blues. **Vinus** (corner of Crosera San Pantalon and San Rocco) is a friendly wine bar serving plates of ham and cheese and occasional live music.

For a late-night ice cream, coffee or liqueur at one of Venice's best *gelaterie*, head to **Paolin** (Campo Santo Stefano), one of the few open very late (until midnight in summer). For a bit of jazz, try the Venice Jazz Club, near Ponte dei Pugni, with a mixture of jazz standards and contemporary tunes (tel: 041-523 2056; www.venicejazzclub.com).

Cannaregio

Fondamenta della Misericordia is the nightlife hub in this northern part of town. Here, lining the once abandoned quaysides, are a cluster of nightspots with atmosphere and fairly decent food. Bustling **Paradiso Perduto** is the liveliest nightspot (tel: 041-720 581; Thur–Sun open until 2am) with live jazz, folk and ethnic music. For traditional Venetian haunts, the alleys off Strada Nova (especially the Campo Santi Apostoli end) conceal excellent *bacari*, such as **Alla Vedova** *(see p.77)* but avoid the charmless tourist traps on Strada Nova itself. The side streets close to the Ca' d'Oro gallery (off Strada Nova) also conceal plenty of traditional bars, as do some of the seemingly bleak quaysides.

San Polo/SantaCroce/Rialto

The Rialto's romantic **Bancogiro** (Campo San Giacometto) is a rather idiosyncratic yet deservedly popular meeting place, especially for pre-dinner or late-night drinks. **Bacaro Jazz**, on the San Marco side of the Rialto Bridge (facing Fondaco dei Tedeschi), is a cocktail bar with jazz videos and occasional live artists. **Osteria Ruga Rialto** (Calle del Sturion 692) offers live jazz, blues and reggae as well as dinner and drinks in a rustic setting. Easybar (Campo Santa Maria Mater Domini; closed Thur) is a cool mix of traditional Venice and contemporary Milan, offering a lounge ambience and a chance to enjoy a classic spritz al bitter. **Novecento** (Campiello Sansoni) doubles as a jazz club and pizzeria.

Above: the bright lights of the Rialto Bridge at night; tray of bellinis.

Dance Clubs

Given the ageing Venetian population, the historic centre of Venice has no recommended dance venues – only a few staid and distinctly old-fashioned nightclubs and one 'disco club'. For brasher and younger nightlife, especially nightclubs, many young Venetians dance the night away with tourists in the clubs on the Lido di Jesolo on the Adriatic coast. (You will need to go there by car, taking a road with a high accident rate.) Mestre, on the mainland, also has some venues, but again, requires a car.

CREDITS

Insight Step by Step Venice
Written by: Susie Boulton and Jessica Stewart, with additional text by Lisa Gerard-Sharp.
Series Editor: Clare Peel
Cartography Editors: Zoë Goodwin, James Macdonald and Neal Jordan-Caws
Picture Manager: Steven Lawrence
Art Editor: Ian Spick
Production: Kenneth Chan
Photography: All pictures © APA Chris Coe, Glyn Genin, Anna Mockford/Nick Bonetti except: AKG London 24; Bridgeman Art Library 44; Corbis 8–9, 46; Fotolibra 2–3, 26–7; iStock-photo 12B, 15B, 20–1, 22, 30B, 35T, 36T, 38–9, 57, 58, 69, 72T, 86, 123; Leonardo 112–13, 113T, 114, 115; Mary Evans 69B; Ros Miller 83, 90T Scala 44–5.
Front cover: main image: 4 Corners; bottom left: iStockphoto; bottom right: Glyn Genin.
Printed by: Insight Print Services (Pte) Ltd, 38 Joo Koon Road, Singapore 628990

DISTRIBUTION

Worldwide
APA Publications GmbH & Co. Verlag KG (Singapore branch)
38 Joo Koon Road
Singapore 628990
Tel: (65) 6865 1600
Fax: (65) 6861 6438

UK and Ireland
GeoCenter International Ltd
Meridian House, Churchill Way West
Basingstoke, Hampshire, RG21 6YR
Tel: (44) 01256 817 987
Fax: (44) 01256 817 988

United States
Langenscheidt Publishers, Inc.
36–36 33rd Street, 4th Floor
Long Island City, NY 11106
Tel: (1) 718 784 0055
Fax: (1) 718 784 0640

Australia
Universal Publishers
1 Waterloo Road, Macquarie Park, NSW 2113
Tel: (61) 2 9857 3700
Fax: (61) 2 9888 9074

New Zealand
Hema Maps New Zealand Ltd (HNZ)
Unit 2, 10 Cryers Road
East Tamaki, Auckland 2013
Tel: (64) 9 273 6459
Fax: (64) 9 273 6479

CONTACTING THE EDITORS

We would appreciate it if readers would alert us to errors or outdated information by writing to us at insight@apaguide.co.uk or APA Publications, PO Box 7910, London SE1 1WE, UK.

www.insightguides.com

INDEX

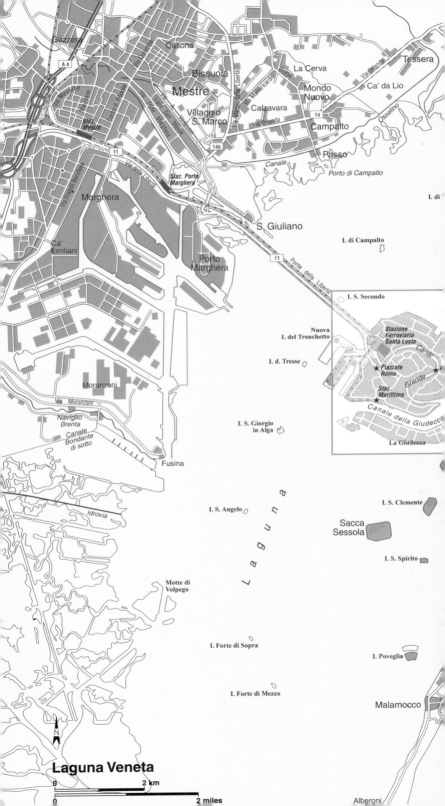